Junior Girl Scout Handbook

Girl Scouts of the U.S.A.
830 Third Avenue
New York, N.Y. 10022

 GIRL SCOUTS OF THE U.S.A.

Betty F Pilsbury, *President*
Frances Hesselbein, *National Executive Director*

Inquiries related to the *Junior Girl Scout Handbook*
should be directed to Program, Girl Scouts of the U.S.A.,
830 Third Avenue, New York, N.Y. 10022.

Credits

Project Coordinator
Joel E. Becker

Director, Program
Sharon Woods Hussey

Manager, Program Development
Harriet S. Mosatche

Director, Graphics and Design
Michael Chanwick

Authors
Harriet S. Mosatche
Sharon Woods Hussey
Damariz Z. Winborne
Verna L. Simpkins
Candace White Ciraco
Toni Eubanks

Cover Design
George Koizumi

Illustrator
Barbara Steadman

How-to Illustrator
Betty de Araujo

Editor
Susan Eno

ISBN 0-88441-336-5
10 9 8 7 6

CONTENTS

Welcome to Junior Girl Scouting   1
Who Am I?   21
Relationships   43
Decisions, Decisions, Decisions   55
Leadership and Groups   65
People   75
Day by Day—Skills for Living   85
Hopes and Dreams   119
Creative Explorations   129
Bridging to Cadette Girl Scouting   163
   Bridge to Cadette Girl Scouts Patch   170

Junior Girl Scout Recognitions   172
   Junior Girl Scout Badges   172
      Leadership   173
      Looking Your Best   174
      Communication   175
      Helping in Your Community   177
      Healthy Living   178
      Technology   179
      Your Outdoor Surroundings   180
      Wider Opportunities   182
      Careers   183
   Junior Girl Scout Signs   184
      Sign of the World   184
Index   186

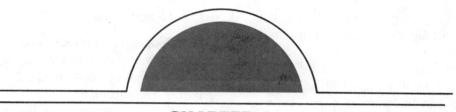

CHAPTER 1

Welcome to Junior Girl Scouting

You've just started a new adventure as a Junior Girl Scout. Whether you are joining Girl Scouting for the first time or have been a member before, you can look forward to enjoying many different activities with friends.

Your friends in Girl Scouting aren't just in your community. Millions of Girl Scouts in the United States, just like you, are having fun planning and doing activities like camping, sports, and games. In fact, all Girl Scouts are part of a worldwide family. Girl Scouting is international—over 100 countries have Girl Scouts or Girl Guides (as they are called in some countries).

Being a Junior Girl Scout

Junior Girl Scouts are usually 9, 10, or 11 years old or in the fourth, fifth, or sixth grade. As a Junior Girl Scout you will have the chance to try many new things, such as horseback riding or working with computers. Besides doing activities just for fun, you can do special activities to earn Girl Scout recognitions—that is, symbols worn on the Girl Scout uniform to show others what you have accomplished. See pages 170 and 172–185 for the recognitions and insignia for Junior Girl Scouts.

Using Your Handbook

Your handbook is full of ideas for fun and adventure. There are many activities that you can plan and do with friends, and some other activities that you probably will want to do on your own. The activities—things to make and things to do—are there to help you learn more about yourself and what is important to you. You have your own talents and skills, and by using those talents and skills, you can make a difference in your own life and in the lives of others.

The *Junior Girl Scout Handbook* can be used to help you in many different kinds of situations. It is your book, so use it in the ways that work best for you. The chapters do not have to be read in any special order. If you meet with other Junior Girl Scouts in a troop or group, look through the handbook and decide on things to do together. Your leader will be a helpful partner for all that you do.

The *Junior Girl Scout Handbook* can also be used to help you complete the many activities in *Girl Scout Badges and Signs*, another resource for Junior Girl Scouts. Both books will help to make your Girl Scout experience the best one possible.

The Girl Scout Promise and Law

As a Girl Scout, you will share a great deal with other Girl Scouts of all ages. Girl Scouts:

- Work together with other Girl Scouts, both girls and adults
- Have pins showing that they are part of a worldwide movement of Girl Scouts and Girl Guides
- Wear a uniform showing their age level and country
- Share traditions, ceremonies, and songs
- Pay national membership dues

The most important thing Girl Scouts share is the Promise and Law. All Girl Scouts—both girls and adults—make the Girl Scout Promise and agree to try to live by the Girl Scout Law.

THE GIRL SCOUT PROMISE

On my honor, I will try:
To serve God and my country,
To help people at all times,
And to live by the Girl Scout Law.

Each line of this Promise has an important meaning.

On my honor, I will try:

When you say this, you are giving your word that you will work hard to live up to the Girl Scout Promise.

To serve God

People in different religious groups think of God in many different ways. As a Girl Scout, you agree to live by your beliefs. How can you live this part of the Promise?

Showing respect for the religious beliefs of others is another important idea in Girl Scouting. Some people's beliefs may be very different from yours. How can you show respect for the religious beliefs of others?

and my country,

As a citizen of the United States, you have many responsibilities to your country. These can include protecting the environment, knowing how the government works, obeying the laws in your community, and helping to make new laws. In what other ways can you show good citizenship?

To help people at all times,

This part of the Promise means that you agree to help others whenever you can. Sometimes you may plan ahead to help others. At other times you may find yourself in an unexpected situation where your assistance is needed. Service to others is very important in Girl Scouting (see pages 72–73).

And to live by the Girl Scout Law.

THE GIRL SCOUT LAW

I will do my best:

- to be honest
- to be fair
- to help where I am needed
- to be cheerful
- to be friendly and considerate
- to be a sister to every Girl Scout
- to respect authority
- to use resources wisely
- to protect and improve the world around me
- to show respect for myself and others through my words and actions.

By trying your best to live each part of the Law, you are doing your best as a Girl Scout. The list below gives some possible ways of doing this. You could add your own ideas to the list.

I will do my best:
to be honest

- Make up a list of times when it's not easy to be honest.
- Describe how you feel when you tell the truth, and how you've felt at times when you didn't.

- _____

- _____

to be fair

- Divide something up in a way that would be fair.
- Design a kaper chart (see page 72).

- _____

- _____

to help where I am needed

- Volunteer to do something at school without being asked.
- Help with a chore in your home.

- _____

- _____

to be cheerful

- Learn to do something to cheer yourself up when you're feeling sad.
- Visit someone who is unable to get outside.

- _____

- _____

to be friendly and considerate

- Do a favor for a friend.
- Learn how to form the friendship circle and give the friendship squeeze (see pages 9–10).

- _____

- _____

to be a sister to every Girl Scout

- Work with another Girl Scout on a badge activity or other project.
- List ways you can be a sister to a Girl Scout from a different culture.

▪ _____

_____

▪ _____

_____

to respect authority

- Make a list of people you respect who are in positions of authority.
- Make a list of ways you can show respect for authority.

▪ _____

_____

▪ _____

_____

to use resources wisely

- Plan an energy, soil, or water conservation week with your troop, other friends, or your family.
- Make something out of a used can, bottle, or cardboard container.

▪ _____

_____

▪ _____

_____

to protect and improve the world around me

- Make a house, feeder, or bath for the birds in your area.
- Organize a clean-up campaign to beautify a littered area in your community.

▪ _____

_____

▪ _____

_____

to show respect for myself and others through my words and actions.

- Decide on something about yourself that you like, and tell a close friend about it.
- Share a family custom with others, and let them know why it has special meaning for you.

▪ _____

_____

▪ _____

_____

People in Girl Scouting

There are many people in Girl Scouting who, together with you, help to make Girl Scouting happen. See the Girl Scout People Pyramid on page 6.

At the top of the pyramid is *you*. Write your name in the blank space. You and millions of other girls—around this country and around the world—are the reasons that Girl Scouting exists.

One way to take part in Girl Scouting is to join a troop. If you are in a Girl Scout troop, put your troop number in the next part of the pyramid. If you are not part of a troop, write in the names of the friends with whom you do Girl Scout activities.

Sometimes adults help you in carrying out Girl Scout activities. Some of the people who do this are Girl Scout leaders—volunteers who work with Girl Scout troops or groups. They help guide meetings, keep records, and find out about events for girls. Write in the names of the adults who work with your troop. If you are not part of a troop, write in the names of those special adults who help you with Girl Scout activities.

Many Girl Scout troops have a leadership team guiding their meetings. There may be leaders, assistant leaders, leaders-in-training, or program aides. All of these people work to make your Girl Scout experiences the very best possible.

To help make Girl Scouting happen in the wider community, groups of people work together in Girl Scout **councils**. There are more than 300 councils in the United States today. Find out the name of your own Girl Scout council and write it on the pyramid. You can wear the name of your council on your uniform sash (see page 13). Invite someone who works in the council office to a Girl Scout meeting to talk about what she does and how the council operates.

Next on the pyramid is Girl Scouts of the U.S.A. (GSUSA), the national organization. The membership dues that you pay to GSUSA each year are

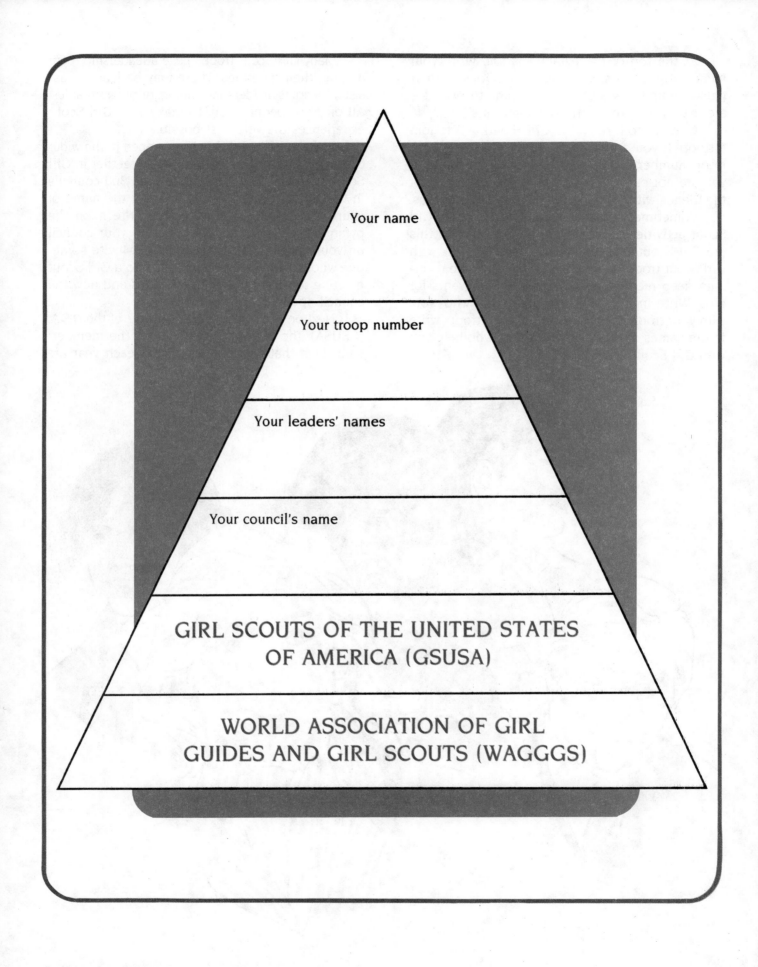

Your name

Your troop number

Your leaders' names

Your council's name

GIRL SCOUTS OF THE UNITED STATES OF AMERICA (GSUSA)

WORLD ASSOCIATION OF GIRL GUIDES AND GIRL SCOUTS (WAGGGS)

used to help people learn about the Girl Scout Movement, which you are part of. GSUSA operates the national centers (see below), publishes books like this handbook, and gets grants for special opportunities and events. GSUSA also coordinates national and international events (wider opportunities) for Cadette and Senior Girl Scouts, and prepares a publication called *Wider Ops: Girl Scout Wider Opportunities* describing these events.

At the base of the pyramid is the World Association of Girl Guides and Girl Scouts (WAGGGS). Your World Association pin shows that you are a part of this worldwide movement; you have about eight million sisters in countries all over the world. Every three years, representatives from this worldwide family meet at a world conference to share ideas and make decisions important to Girl Guides and Girl Scouts everywhere.

The longer you stay in Girl Scouting, the more people in the Girl Scout People Pyramid you will meet. You will discover that you are an important part of a very important family.

The National Centers

There are two Girl Scout national centers, each with its own special focus and activities. These centers are operated by Girl Scouts of the U.S.A.

Juliette Gordon Low Girl Scout National Center is the childhood home of the founder of Girl Scouting in the United States. Over 400 troops a year travel from all over the country to visit this home where Juliette Gordon Low was born, in order to participate in special programs offered there. More than 2,500 Junior Girl Scouts tour the center annually. There they can learn more about Juliette

Juliette Gordon Low Girl Scout National Center

Edith Macy Conference Center

Low and her work with the Girl Scouts, about the Gordon family and their home, and about many other interesting aspects of nineteenth-century life. Since this center is also a public museum, many people besides Girl Scouts come to visit, including individual Girl Scouts traveling with their families. For more information about travel to the center with a troop or as an individual, write to Juliette Gordon Low Girl Scout National Center, 142 Bull Street, Savannah, Georgia 31401.

Edith Macy Conference Center is 35 miles from midtown New York City in Briarcliff Manor, New York. Adults in Girl Scouting come to this center for training courses, in which they learn ways to help make your Girl Scout experiences the best possible. They can use the classrooms, auditorium, library, swimming pool, and nature trails. Adults in Girl Scouting may also come to the Girl Scout Outdoor Education Center, which is part of the Edith Macy Conference Center. There, they can learn more about camping and outdoor activities for Girl Scouts. The center serves as a training and testing site for many new ideas and types of equipment that can be used in Girl Scout councils across the country.

The World Centers

There are four international world centers where older Girl Guides and Girl Scouts from all over the world can meet: Our Cabaña in Mexico, Our Chalet in Switzerland, Olave Centre in England, and Sangam in India. For more information, write to Program Group, Girl Scouts of the U.S.A., 830 Third Avenue, New York, New York 10022.

Our Chalet

Olave Centre

Our Cabaña

Sangam

Girl Scout Traditions

Girl Scouts and Girl Guides all around the world share special signs, a handshake, the friendship squeeze, a motto, and a slogan.

The **Girl Scout sign** is made by raising three fingers of the right hand. This sign stands for the three parts of the Promise. You give the sign when:

- you say the Promise
- you are welcomed into Girl Scouting at an investiture ceremony
- you receive a patch or badge
- you greet other Girl Scouts and Girl Guides

The **Girl Scout handshake** is a more formal way of greeting other Girl Scouts and Girl Guides. You shake hands with the left hand and give the Girl Scout sign with your right hand.

The **quiet sign** is used in meetings and other gatherings to quiet a group. The sign is made by raising your right hand high. As people in the group see the quiet sign, they stop talking and also raise their hands. Once everyone is silent, the meeting continues.

Sometimes, perhaps in a meeting or around a campfire, Girl Scouts and Girl Guides form a **friendship circle**. The circle stands for an unbroken chain of friendship with Girl Scouts and Girl Guides all around the world. Girls and their leaders

stand in a circle. Each person crosses her right arm over her left and clasps hands with her friends on both sides. Everyone is silent as a **friendship squeeze** is passed from hand to hand. When you are part of a friendship circle, you can feel its meaning. Form a friendship circle with the girls in your group and try the friendship squeeze.

The **Girl Scout motto** is "Be prepared." It means that Girl Scouts learn how to do things ahead of time, so they will be ready and able to deal with whatever situation arises. For example, you learn first-aid skills so that you will know how to take care of yourself or someone else who is hurt or sick. Learning new skills such as these is part of the fun of Junior Girl Scouting.

At right is the motto in some other languages. Tips on pronunciation are given in parentheses.

The **Girl Scout slogan** is "Do a good turn daily." Note that a good turn doesn't have to involve a lot of effort or time. It might just be a small courtesy or favor for another person.

A Girl Scout service project is a type of good turn that takes planning and time. See pages 72–73 for more information.

Arabic	كوني مستعدة (Koony mostaeda)	Be prepared
French	Toujours prête (Too zhoor prêt)	Always ready
Hebrew	הֱיֵה נָכוֹן (Hay yeh na khown)	Be prepared
Korean	준비 (June bee)	Be prepared
Spanish	Siempre lista (See em pray lees tah)	Always ready

The Girl Scout Troop

Part of the fun of Girl Scouting is sharing experiences with girls your age. You might be part of a group called the Girl Scout troop.

A troop works in much the same way as a democratic country—it has a system of government in which all the members (or their representatives) work together. They make decisions, select leaders, and make sure that everyone's feelings and interests are taken into account. Each member is given an equal chance to say what she feels the troop ought to do. Sometimes, decisions are made by taking a vote.

The troop government system is set up and run by the girl members in partnership with adult leaders. When choosing a form of government, you and the other girls in the troop might begin by discussing the different possible systems (see pages 69–70). Then you can pick one that best meets the needs and interests of the girls in your troop.

Age Levels

Any girl who is 5 through 17 years old or in kindergarten through the twelfth grade can become a Girl Scout in the United States. Girls of different races, cultures, and religious groups are part of the Girl Scout Movement. Every Girl Scout must make the Girl Scout Promise and try to live by the Girl Scout Law.

Girl Scouts of different ages wear different uni-

GIRL SCOUTING AT THE FIVE AGE LEVELS

	Age or Grade	Form of Troop Government	Recognitions
Daisy	5–6 years old or in kindergarten or first grade	Daisy Girl Scout Circle	Certificate when Daisy Girl Scout year is begun and completed
Brownie	6–8 years old or in first, second, or third grade	Brownie Girl Scout Ring with committee	Brownie Girl Scout Try-Its Bridge to Junior Girl Scouts patch Dabbler badge
Junior	8–11 years old or in third, fourth, fifth, or sixth grade	Patrol system, executive board, or town meeting	Badges (Dabbler, green, tan, white) Signs (Rainbow, Sun, Satellite, World) Junior Aide patch Bridge to Cadette Girl Scouts patch
Cadette	11–14 years old or in sixth, seventh, eighth, or ninth grade	Patrol system, executive board, or town meeting	Interest project patches From Dreams to Reality patch or From Dreams to Reality pilots pin Silver Leadership Award Gold Leadership Award Volunteer Service bars Challenge of Being a Girl Scout
Senior	14–17 years old or in ninth, tenth, eleventh, or twelfth grade	Patrol system, executive board, or other form of government developed by troop	Challenge of Living the Promise and Law Girl Scout Silver Award Ten-Year Award* Girl Scout Gold Award*

*For Senior Girl Scouts only.

forms. They take part in group activities in troops, camps, and council programs. Sometimes they come together to work on projects and to do bridging activities. (See pages 163–171 to find out about bridging.)

The chart on page 11 shows the five different age levels in Girl Scouting.

The Girl Scout Uniform

A uniform is a privilege of membership enjoyed by Girl Scouts and Girl Guides around the world. You might decide to buy the uniform that has been designed just for Junior Girl Scouts.

On some occasions, it will be important to wear your Girl Scout uniform. You may want to wear it at meetings, when you participate in ceremonies, when you travel as a Girl Scout, when you attend an event as part of a Girl Scout group, and when you attend church, temple, or synagogue on a special Girl Scout day.

Girl Scout Insignia and Recognitions

Girl Scout insignia are the badges, pins, and special identifications that you may wear on your uniform. Some of your Girl Scout insignia must be earned—you will need to do special activities in order to get them. These are called recognitions. Girl Scout badges and signs are examples of insignia that are also recognitions. You can earn recognitions by doing the activities described in *Girl Scout Badges and Signs* and in the "Junior Girl Scout Recognitions" chapter in this handbook.

Many religious groups have special recognitions for Girl Scouts of their faith. If you wish to earn one of these recognitions, your Girl Scout council, Girl Scout leader, or religious group can tell you more about it.

Your Girl Scout pin is a symbol of your membership in Girl Scouting. Its trefoil shape represents the three parts of the Girl Scout Promise. There are two versions of the membership pin. The newer one has three profiles inside the trefoil to show that the Girl Scout organization is a contemporary one based on timeless values—an organization that points girls toward the future and shows them the many opportunities open to them. The dark and light profiles represent the diversity of Girl Scout membership and symbolize Girl Scouting's focus as an organization open to all girls. The traditional version of the pin has the initials "G S" inside the trefoil, along with the American eagle and shield that are part of the Great Seal of the United States of America. On the shield are 13 stripes which represent the 13 original states, while the horizontal bar across the top of the stripes stands for Congress binding all the states together. The eagle faces right—the position of honor. He holds arrows—a symbol of power, and an olive branch— a symbol of peace.

Your blue and gold World Association pin shows that you are part of a worldwide movement of Girl Guides and Girl Scouts. The blue stands for the sky and the gold stands for the sun. The trefoil stands for the three parts of the Girl Scout Promise. The base of the trefoil is shaped like a flame, which represents the love of humankind and the flame that burns in the hearts of Girl Guides and Girl Scouts around the world. The line in the middle of the trefoil stands for the compass needle that guides us, while the two stars stand for the Promise and Law.

Girl Scout membership pin shows that you are a Girl Scout in the United States of America.

Troop number and troop crest show what Girl Scout troop you belong to.

Council strip shows what council your troop is part of.

Girl Scouts of the U.S.A. strip shows that you are part of the Girl Scout family in the United States of America.

World Association pin shows that you belong to the worldwide movement of Girl Guides and Girl Scouts.

Brownie Girl Scout wings show that you flew up from Brownie to Junior Girl Scouting.

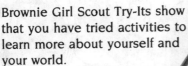

Brownie Girl Scout Try-Its show that you have tried activities to learn more about yourself and your world.

Bridge to Junior Girl Scouts patch shows that you completed bridging activities during your last year as a Brownie Girl Scout.

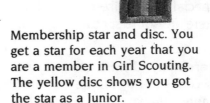

Membership star and disc. You get a star for each year that you are a member in Girl Scouting. The yellow disc shows you got the star as a Junior.

Junior Aide patch shows that you have helped prepare girls for Junior Girl Scouting.

Junior Girl Scout Signs—the Rainbow, the Sun, the Satellite, and the World—show that you have done some special activities.

Girl Scout badges show that you have done activities to build various skills.

Bridge to Cadette Girl Scouts patch shows that you spent part of your last year as a Junior Girl Scout doing things that will help you "cross the bridge" to Cadette Girl Scouting.

Girl Scout Ceremonies

A ceremony is an act or celebration that honors someone or means something important to the participants. Girl Scout ceremonies can be short and part of a regular meeting, or they can take up nearly the whole meeting.

Ceremonies may include girls in your troop, other girls in Girl Scouting, Girl Scout leaders or other adults, and special guests like parents, relatives, and friends. Here are some special Girl Scout ceremonies:

- **Investiture ceremony.** Girl Scouts welcome someone into Girl Scouting for the first time.
- **Fly-up ceremony.** Brownie Girl Scouts become Junior Girl Scouts.
- **Bridging ceremony.** Girl Scouts "cross the bridge" to the next age level. See pages 163–171 for more about bridging.

- **Rededication ceremony.** Girl Scouts renew their dedication to the Girl Scout Promise and Law. This ceremony can take place anytime, but is usually held at the beginning or end of the troop year.
- **Court of Awards.** Girl Scouts receive recognitions and other insignia.
- **Girl Scouts' Own.** A special ceremony created by a troop or group around a theme. The purpose is for the girls and leaders to show how they feel about the theme. The ceremony may include readings, songs, poetry, drama, and so forth.

The following types of ceremonies—candlelight ceremonies and flag ceremonies—can take place on their own, or can take place as part of another ceremony or celebration.

CANDLELIGHT CEREMONIES

A candle lighting helps remind people about the meaning of the Girl Scout Promise and Law.

FLAG CEREMONIES

Many ceremonies include a flag ceremony, which honors the American flag as the symbol of our country. Your troop might have a flag ceremony—

- as part of an investiture, rededication, fly-up, or Court of Awards ceremony
- as part of a ceremony on a Girl Scouting special day
- as a way to open or close a troop meeting or camp day
- at a community ceremony or celebration

At a flag ceremony, you say the **Pledge of Allegiance:**

I pledge allegiance to the flag of the United States of America and to the Republic for which it stands, one nation under God, indivisible, with liberty and justice for all.

You might also sing a patriotic song and repeat the Girl Scout Promise and Law as part of the flag ceremony.

Flying the Flag

We show respect for our country's flag in many ways. A public law, passed by Congress, describes how everyone should treat the flag.

The most important thing to remember is that when you fly the American flag in the United States, you always give it the position of honor. You put it either in front of other flags, higher than other flags, or to the right of other flags. (If you were to hold the flag while facing the people who will see it, your right side would be the flag's own right.) In the United States, when a group of flags are together, no flag is ever larger or flown higher than the American flag.

make sure the blue part is at the top and on the flag's own right.

3. Never use the flag as a cover or place anything on top of it. Make sure the flag never touches the floor or ground.

4. Keep the flag clean.

5. When a flag gets old and is too worn to use, do not throw it in the trash. Instead, it should be destroyed. The best way is to give it to an adult to be burned.

6. The right way to fold the flag is shown below.

Holding a Flag Ceremony

Every flag ceremony has a **color guard,** a team that carries and guards the flags. The term "color guard" came to be used because the American flag is sometimes called "the colors"; however, a color guard may carry and guard other flags as well. The girls who carry the flags are called "flag bearers." The girls who stand beside the flags are called "guards." There is also a Girl Scout-in-charge, whose job is to announce each part of the ceremony.

Saluting the Flag

You stand at attention and salute by placing your right hand over your heart—

- when the flag is being raised or lowered
- when the flag passes you in a parade
- when you say the Pledge of Allegiance
- when "The Star-Spangled Banner," the American national anthem, is played

People salute only the flag of their own country. If you are ever in a situation where people from another country are saluting their flag, just stand at attention.

Tips for Handling the Flag

1. Fly the flag only from sunrise until sunset. However, it can be flown at night if a spotlight is on it. Do not fly it in bad weather unless it is an all-weather flag.

2. When you hang the flag on a wall or in a window where people will see it from the street,

Here are some steps that your troop might follow in a flag ceremony:

1. The girls stand in a horseshoe. The Girl Scout-in-charge says, "Color guard, fall out." The color guard goes to where the flags are.

2. The flag bearers salute the flags and pick them up. The American flag is always lifted first. The girls carrying the flags stand side by side. The guards stand on either side of the girls.

3. The Girl Scout-in-charge says, "Color guard, advance." The color guard marches to the open end of the horseshoe. Everyone stands at attention.

4. Members of the color guard stand silently throughout the ceremony because their job is to carry and guard the flag. All the other Girl Scouts salute the flag.

5. The Girl Scout-in-charge leads the Pledge of Allegiance. She says, "Girl Scouts, the flag of your country. Pledge allegiance."

6. The Girl Scout-in-charge says, "Color guard, retire the colors." The color guard leaves the horseshoe and carries the flags back to their stands or to the place where they are stored.

7. If the flags are placed in stands, the guards help the flag bearers. The American flag is the last one placed. The color guard salutes the American flag and returns to the troop.

The ceremony ends when the color guard is out of sight of the troop or when it puts the flags away.

PLANNING A CEREMONY

By doing a good job of planning, you can make your ceremony as meaningful as possible. Basically, any ceremony has three parts—the opening, the main part, and the closing. Look over the checklist below for possible things to include:

Opening

This introduction to the ceremony can be very brief. For example:

- Welcome guests.
- Tell the purpose of the ceremony.
- Set the mood. Will your ceremony be quiet, happy, serious?

Main Part

This is the central part of the ceremony and can involve many different types of words or actions. For example:

- Sing songs.
- Recite poems.
- Read special words and sayings.
- Tell stories.
- Act out a story.
- Honor the flag.
- Say the Girl Scout Promise and Law.
- Light candles.

Closing

This part, which ends the ceremony, could include some meaningful parting words or acts. For example:

- Thank-yous to special guests.
- A closing song or poem.
- Goodbyes to everyone who attended.

Juliette Gordon Low, Founder of Girl Scouting in the United States

Girl Scouting was started in the United States in 1912 by a woman named Juliette Gordon Low. Juliette's uncle gave her the nickname Daisy when she was born, and all her life her friends knew her as Daisy.

Daisy (Juliette) was born in Savannah, Georgia, on Halloween—October 31, 1860—a few months before the start of the Civil War between the North and South. Daisy had three sisters and two brothers. Their father was in the cotton business and their mother ran the household.

As a young girl, Daisy kept herself very busy. She formed clubs, rode horses, invented games, played tennis, wrote, acted in and produced plays, and started a children's magazine. One of her clubs, called "The Helpful Hands," was a sewing club that made useful things for the poor.

Daisy loved animals. She was a very good horseback rider and she had a parrot named Polly Poons. Once she saved a kitten from drowning in a flood. Another time, she wrapped a cow in blankets taken from the guest bedroom to keep the animal from getting cold. Daisy's mother wasn't very happy about this, though, because the cow walked all over the blankets.

Daisy studied at a boarding school. She was a good student in some subjects but weak in other subjects, such as spelling. Her favorite subject was art, especially drawing, and she continued her artistic interests throughout her life. She painted, sculpted, and did metal work—for example, she made a set of wrought iron gates for her home.

Daisy's life was not free of problems. When she was 25, she developed an earache. Against her doctor's advice, she insisted that he treat it with silver nitrate, which she had read was a remedy for earache. As a result of the attempted treatment, Daisy lost her hearing in one ear. A year later, on her wedding day, as the guests threw rice for good luck, a grain fell into her other ear. The doctors' efforts to treat the injury were not successful, and Daisy became totally deaf in that ear. But Daisy was not stopped by her disabilities.

Daisy married a man named William Low. After the wedding they went to live in England and Scotland, where they remained for many years. However, their marriage was not a happy one, and Daisy was in the process of getting a divorce when her

husband died. Although they never had any children, Daisy liked children very much and especially enjoyed helping girls.

While Daisy was living in Scotland, she met a man named Sir (later he was given the title of Lord) Robert Baden-Powell, who was the founder of Boy Scouting. Lord Baden-Powell and his sister, Agnes, started Girl Guiding because they found that many girls were interested in hiking, learning about the outdoors, learning survival skills, working on achievement badges, serving their community, and doing activities as a group. Daisy Low thought Girl Guiding was a very worthwhile program. For a while, she led girls in Girl Guiding in England and Scotland. When she returned to Savannah after her husband died, she decided to give girls in the United States the opportunity to join in the new adventure. With the help of her cousin, Nina Pape, Daisy started the first American Girl Guide troop. (Later the name in the United States was changed to Girl Scouts.) Daisy had called Nina on the telephone and said, "Come right over! I've got something for the girls of Savannah, and all America, and all the world, and we're going to start it tonight!"

On March 12, 1912, eighteen girls met with Daisy to form the first two troops. (That's why March 12 is the Girl Scout birthday.) The girls learned the Girl Guide Law, played games, took nature hikes, went bird watching, learned first aid, went camping, learned to sew, and helped other people. The girls made their own uniforms—long, dark blue skirts and blouses with light blue ties. They also made their own badges. When other troops were formed, they started an intertroop basketball league.

Daisy felt that camping and outdoor life should be important parts of Girl Scouting, and she spent a lot of her own money to make sure that girls had places to camp. Camp Lowlands, in Georgia, was the first official Girl Scout camp in the United States. Many of the girls in Daisy's first troop went camping there.

Very soon after Daisy began the first troop in 1912, Girl Scouting started to spread throughout the country. Juliette worked hard to make sure that girls in the United States could become part of Girl Scouting and would know they were sisters to all the Girl Guides and Girl Scouts in other parts of the world.

Juliette Gordon Low died in 1927. A few months after she died, the Juliette Low World Friendship Fund was started. The fund is designed to honor her and her vision of worldwide friendship. Every year, Girl Scouts all over the United States give money to this fund—usually on Juliette Low's birthday, on Thinking Day (the birthday of Lord and Lady Baden-Powell), or during Girl Scout Week. Some of the money in the Juliette Low World Friendship Fund is used to send Girl Scouts to other countries and to bring girls to the United States. The rest goes to the Thinking Day Fund set up by the World Association of Girl Guides and Girl Scouts to help it carry out projects around the world.

Few women have been as highly honored by the United States government as Juliette Low. During World War II, the government named a liberty ship after her. In 1948, a Juliette Gordon Low U.S. postage stamp was printed, and in 1973, her portrait was presented to the National Gallery in Washington, D.C. In 1974, Daisy was also honored

by her own state of Georgia, when a bust of her was placed in the Georgia State Capitol Hall of Fame. In 1983, Congress designated that a new government office building in Savannah, Georgia, be named after the founder of Girl Scouting. It is called the Juliette Gordon Low Federal Complex.

Juliette Gordon Low is remembered as a woman who worked for peace and good will. Her dream was to have young people make the world a friendly, peaceful place. She wanted young people to have a greater understanding of themselves and others. To help achieve this, she wanted to give something special to girls in the United States—and that was Girl Scouting.

Some Interesting Facts About Girl Scout History

- The first American Girl Scout was Daisy Gordon Lawrence, Juliette Low's niece.
- The first Girl Scout handbook was published in 1913.
- The first nationwide celebration of Girl Scout Week was held in 1919.
- The first national Girl Scout cookie sale was held in 1936.
- Beginning in 1938, there were three age levels of Girl Scouts: Brownie Girl Scouts, ages 7–9; Intermediate Girl Scouts, ages 10–13; and Senior Girl Scouts, ages 14–17.
- In 1963, the age levels were changed—Girl Scouts were divided into Brownie, Junior, Cadette, and Senior age levels.
- In 1984, the Girl Scout family grew again. Now there are five age levels of Girl Scouts—Daisy, Brownie, Junior, Cadette, and Senior Girl Scouts.

Girl Scouting's Special Days

Girl Scouts have three special birthdays to celebrate:

- OCTOBER 31—Juliette Gordon Low's birthday (also known as Founder's Day).
- FEBRUARY 22—Thinking Day, the birthday of both Lord Baden-Powell and Lady Baden-Powell.
- MARCH 12—The birthday of Girl Scouting in the United States.
- APRIL 22—Girl Scout Leader's Day.

The Worlds of Interest

As a Girl Scout, you'll be having a wide variety of experiences. The activities in which you participate can be grouped into large subject areas called worlds of interest.

The **World of Well-Being** has activities and information that can help you to be a happy and healthy person. Keeping yourself safe and sound, learning about how you grow, and developing yourself to be the best that you can be are things you will explore in this world.

The **World of People** focuses on everyone who shares the world with you—family, friends, people from your community, people who have different cultures and backgrounds. The activities in this world include learning ways to help people and to make the world a better place.

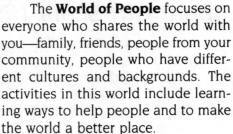

The **World of Today and Tomorrow** helps you to find out more about the "whys" of things today and the "what ifs" of tomorrow. This world is experiments and discoveries. It means learning more about what is happening now so you can be ready for tomorrow.

Activities in the **World of the Arts** can be anything from architectural drawing to xylophone playing. This world includes art for all your senses. You also can learn about the important ways in which art enriches everyone's lives.

The **World of the Out-of-Doors** is about you and your environment, the plants and creatures you share the earth with, and all the things that help protect and improve the natural world.

Alongside each activity description in this handbook, you will see a symbol that tells you which world of interest the activity explores. The color of each box matches the color code for each world of interest.

- ■ Red = Well-Being
- ■ Blue = People
- ■ Orange = Today and Tomorrow
- ■ Purple = Arts
- ■ Yellow = Out-of-Doors

Sometimes, an activity can help you to learn about more than one world. For example, if you see this symbol ■ ■ you know that the activity focuses on both the World of Well-Being and the World of Today and Tomorrow. When you are working on Junior Girl Scout recognitions, check the symbol because it will help you to keep track of what you have done.

Suzy Safety

Another symbol you will come across throughout this book is Suzy Safety. The symbol is a reminder to do things the safe way.

CHAPTER 2

Who Am I?

Growing up is an exciting experience because you keep changing in so many ways—the way you look, the way you think, the way you feel. As you get older, keep thinking of yourself in the following way:

> There is no one in the world like Me.
> No one has My talents, dreams, or hopes.
> No one can take My place.

The One and Only—Me!

Everything that has ever happened to you, from learning to tie your shoelaces to becoming a Girl Scout, has helped to shape you into the person you are. In many ways, you may be very similar to other girls your age. You may share the same interests or wear the same kinds of clothes. But no one else is quite like you. See for yourself:

■ ■ Write an advertisement for someone to replace you. In your ad, list the qualities you have that you feel are most important. You might in-clude some of the things you like and don't like to do, a special place you have always wanted to visit, your favorite animal, food, or sport. You can also list information about your family. The finished ad might look something like this:

> *Wanted*: Someone to be me for a day. Must love animals, especially large dogs like German shepherds. Must like to sing—but only when washing dishes or roller skating. Must be able to help my younger sisters with their math homework, and be good at putting on puppet shows for them when they're bored. Must like to collect record albums, articles about travel, and rocks. Must love lasagna and hate turkey wings.

After you have written your advertisement, try to think of someone who can take your place. You probably can't find anyone who even comes close!

Sharing advertisements like these is a great way to learn more about your friends. After each person writes an advertisement for herself, place all the advertisements in a paper bag. Shake the bag. Have each person pick one and read it aloud

to the group. The group then tries to guess who the person is.

■ ■ CREATE AN IMAGE BOOK This is a scrapbook that describes your special personal qualities—who you are, what you like or want, what you hope to be. At the top of each page, write a statement that says something positive about you. For example, you might write "I am kind." Then, everything else on that page would be about kindness—you might cut out magazine pictures of people being kind to animals, to older people, to children, to the land. The second page might be headed "I like seashells" and could be filled with photos of seashells. The third page might be titled "I enjoy traveling" and could have maps, countries, foreign words, names of places, photos taken in other countries. Whenever you think of a new way of describing yourself, just add a page to your Image Book.

How Do Others See You?

There are many different ways you can look at yourself. How do you think others see you? Fill in the blanks.

My family thinks that I _____

_____

_____

_____

My best friend thinks that I _____

_____

_____

My teacher thinks that I _____

_____

_____

_____

Often, people don't see you in quite the same way you see yourself. Since others don't know you as well as you know yourself, they can be mistaken in their ideas about you. So, don't base your view of yourself too much on what other people think. Get to know the real you!

She's smart and has many good ideas.

She's a great friend. We have lots of fun together.

She's an average student. Her grades would be better if she'd work a little harder.

What's Important to You?

Values are those things we hold dearest. Your values are shaped by many things—your family, your religious beliefs, your peers, your own experiences. People's values often change as they grow older and are affected by new experiences.

■ In this activity, you have to make value judgments—that is, decisions in which you think about what people, ideas, or things mean the most to you. As you answer each question below, consider what values led you to make the choice you did.

1. What living person do you most admire?

_____

Why? _____

2. What do you like most about your best friend?

_____

Why? _____

3. What do you enjoy most about Girl Scouting?

_____

Why? _____

4. What one thing would you save if your home caught on fire?

_____

Why? _____

5. Who is your favorite character in a book, movie, or television show?

_____

Why? _____

6. What is one thing you really believe in?

_____

Why? _____

7. What one thing would you like to do better?

_____

Why? _____

You can find out even more about your values by taking this quiz:

VALUES QUIZ

■ How important are each of these to you? Be honest in answering and don't check "Very Important" for every item.

	Very Important	Important	A Little Important	Not Important
1. Playing with friends	_____	_____	_____	_____
2. Solving a problem on your own	_____	_____	_____	_____
3. Being president of your class at school	_____	_____	_____	_____
4. Participating in the services of your religious group	_____	_____	_____	_____

	Very Important	Important	A Little Important	Not Important
5. Having expensive clothes	_____	_____	_____	_____
6. Discovering something no one else has ever known	_____	_____	_____	_____
7. Learning a great deal about a subject that interests you	_____	_____	_____	_____
8. Doing a service project	_____	_____	_____	_____
9. Earning more badges than anyone you know	_____	_____	_____	_____
10. Traveling to new places	_____	_____	_____	_____
11. Being in charge of a group	_____	_____	_____	_____
12. Celebrating religious holidays	_____	_____	_____	_____
13. Being close to your family	_____	_____	_____	_____
14. Becoming famous someday	_____	_____	_____	_____
15. Doing exciting things	_____	_____	_____	_____
16. Having a high-paying job	_____	_____	_____	_____
17. Taking care of a baby	_____	_____	_____	_____
18. Spending time with your family	_____	_____	_____	_____
19. Having close friends	_____	_____	_____	_____
20. Being able to freely choose what you will do	_____	_____	_____	_____

Here's what the different items in the quiz mean:

Items 1 and 19 represent the value of having and being with friends.

Items 2 and 20 represent the value of independence, the importance of making your own decisions.

Items 3 and 11 represent the value of power, the importance of being in a leadership role.

Items 4 and 12 represent religious or spiritual values.

Items 5 and 16 represent the value of money.

Items 6 and 7 represent the value of knowledge.

Items 8 and 17 represent the value of helping others.

Items 9 and 14 represent the value of gaining recognition for what you do.

Items 10 and 15 represent the value of adventure.

Items 13 and 18 represent the value of having close family ties.

By looking at the items that you checked as "Very Important," you will get some idea of what things mean the most to you. You may value several things very highly—for instance, family, knowledge, friends, and adventure. This means that you'll probably have to make many choices in life. The "Decisions, Decisions, Decisions" chapter can be of help.

■ Read about Lorraine and see how she made a decision based upon her values.

Lorraine's Values

For several years, Lorraine, Holly, Carmen, and Linda had been very good friends. But now they were all living in different towns. Holly had moved away when her parents divorced. Carmen's family moved when her mother's company relocated. Linda's family left the community after her father lost his job. Only Lorraine was still living in the Parkside neighborhood.

When Lorraine found out that Holly, Carmen, and Linda were all going to be in town on May 7 for a school reunion, she was very excited. She knew it would be fun to talk about their old teachers, compare notes on the boys they had met, and see how each girl had changed. But then Lorraine remembered that May 7 was her mom's birthday and her dad had planned a special party. Mom had been quite ill during the past year, and now that she was getting better, this birthday party was going to be an important celebration. Lorraine decided that she would pass up her school reunion to be at her mom's party. Lorraine's decision had been hard to make, since friendship and family were both important to her.

OTHER ACTIVITIES RELATING TO VALUES

■■ With your friends, act out skits about the following. (Or think up your own ideas and act them out.)

- A girl who values doing well in school more than anything else.

- A conflict between wanting to help others and wanting lots of money.

■ Identify the values in the Girl Scout Promise and Law. Discuss them with others.

■ Think of types of values that are not in the Values Quiz on pages 25–26. Add some items of your own to the quiz.

■ Ask other people, perhaps your friends or family members, to take the Values Quiz. Compare their answers to yours and discuss similarities and differences.

■■ Match types of values with different career choices. For example, the value of power might be matched with a career in politics, and the value of schooling and knowledge might be matched with a career in science. Read the "Hopes and Dreams" chapter for more information.

Appreciating Your Talents

■ You already know how to do hundreds of things, and you'll learn hundreds more as you get older.

You may not talk much about your skills and talents because you don't want others to think you're bragging. But today is your day to brag. Finish these "proud of" statements:

1. I am proud that I can _____

_____

2. I am proud that I decided to _____

_____

3. I am proud that I made _____

_____

4. I am proud that I made my friends or family happy by _____

_____

5. I am proud of these special talents and abilities:

_____

_____

_____

Now, think of things you would like to improve on or learn.

1. I would like to be better at _____

_____

2. I could make my family happier if I _____

_____

3. I would like to learn how to _____

_____

4. I would be a better friend if I _____

_____

5. Something I could work on now to improve my community (or the world) is _____

_____

■■ To help you change a problem into something to be proud of, try the "Planning to Reach a Goal" activity on pages 123–124.

Interests and Hobbies

There are a great many hobbies you could enjoy doing in your free time. A hobby can last a lifetime—many adults still enjoy hobbies they started as children. Here are some ideas for hobbies.

COLLECTING AS A HOBBY

The list of things that can be collected is endless. Some are:

Model airplanes or cars	Dolls
Recipes	Records
Baseball cards	Shells
Stickers	Stamps
Coins	

CREATING AS A HOBBY

You might start a hobby that fits with your particular creative interests or talents. You may need lessons to learn how to do the activity well. Probably, you will find that the more you work at your hobby, the better you get. Some people have even turned their hobbies into paying jobs. Some examples of these kinds of hobbies are:

Dancing	Building things
Singing	Acting
Playing a musical instrument	Painting
	Cooking
Sewing or embroidering	Writing short stories
Taking photographs	

SPORTS AND GAMES AS A HOBBY

These days, girls can participate in practically any sport or game that interests them. Here are a few:

Basketball	Swimming
Softball	Acrobatics
Chess or other board games	Soccer
	Skating
Card games	

OUTDOOR ACTIVITIES AS A HOBBY

What do you most enjoy doing in the out-of-doors? Here are some popular activities:

Hiking	Bicycling
Bird watching	Walking
Camping	Jogging
Fishing	Kite flying
Gardening	

OTHER HOBBIES

Do you have some hobbies that don't fit into any of the above categories? To give just a few examples, many people enjoy reading, working with a computer, canning fruits and vegetables, repairing bicycles, window shopping. Make a list of your own favorite hobbies.

HOBBIES CAN BECOME CAREERS

Sometimes hobbies develop into careers. Here are some examples:

Hobby or Interest	Career
Acrobatics	Stunt person
Sewing	Fashion designer, wardrobe consultant
Building things	Architect, carpenter
Repairing things	Auto mechanic, electrician
Model airplanes	Pilot, flight attendant
Computers	Computer programmer, word processor
Writing	Speech writer, editor
Photography	Photographer, television camera operator
Art	Artist, book illustrator
Music	Musician, musical director
Cooking	Chef, dietician

■■■■ You can do more with your hobbies by earning the "Hobbies and Pets" badge in *Girl Scout Badges and Signs*.

Exploring and Understanding Your Feelings

Feelings affect the way you act and the way you think about yourself and others. Your feelings are always changing—you may be happy one minute and sad the next. The feelings you have in a given situation may be the same as or different from the feelings of others who are present.

Sometimes, you express your feelings with parts of your body, such as your eyes or hands. People very often try to hide their feelings. But in many cases, letting your feelings show can help you feel better and can make it easier for you to get along with others.

The activities in this section can help you to learn more about your feelings and how they affect you and others.

■■ Make a poster or write a poem that expresses how you feel.

■■ Choose a situation and act it out in front of your friends. Use your face and body to show how you might feel in that situation—no talking. Have other girls guess the feeling you are trying to express.

■ What feelings do you think are being expressed by the four people in the picture below?

■■ Keep a diary of your feelings for a week. Each day, write down how you feel and why.

■■ Talk or write about healthy ways to express your feelings, such as telling someone how you feel or crying if you want to.

■ Read the descriptions in the next column and think about how you would feel in each situation. Choose a feeling word (or words) from the list and write it (them) in the blank space. There are no "right" answers. You may use a feeling word more than once, and you may use more than one word for each situation.

Feeling words: Angry, Afraid, Happy, Sad, Lonely, Jealous, Proud, Worried, Disappointed, Loved, Eager, Frustrated, Embarrassed, Surprised, Excited

1. The adult who cares for you is in the hospital.

2. Your best friend is moving away.

3. You fall off your bicycle.

4. You don't get what you want for your birthday.

5. You earn your first badge.

6. School is closed because of a snowstorm.

7. Your favorite pet dies.

8. Your favorite TV program is about to start when your television set breaks down.

9. You accidentally leave your book bag on the bus.

10. You receive a special gift in the mail.

11. You have an important test in math tomorrow.

12. You win the school essay contest.

13. You are waiting to see if you got a part in the school play.

14. Someone is following you down a dark street.

Tracy's Column

Dealing with your feelings can be difficult. Sometimes having someone to talk to or give you advice can be very helpful. You might be able to find someone like Tracy who takes the time to offer her advice to young people. On page 33 are some letters that Tracy received, along with her answers.

Dear Tracy,
My mom left my dad when I was seven years old (I'm ten now) because he drank too much and sometimes he treated her badly. Now we live far away from him. I never see him anymore and I miss him. My mom is busy working all day, and at night she's too tired to spend time with my brother and me. Sometimes I feel like I don't have any parents. What should I do?

Lonely and Confused

Dear Lonely and Confused,
There are a number of things you could do to improve your situation. First of all, let your mother know how you feel. You could offer to help her more at home so she will have some time to do things with you and your brother. If she doesn't work on weekends, plan an activity that the three of you can do together. You could also write to your father. The two of you might form a friendship by mail. Thanks for sharing your feelings with me.

Tracy

Dear Tracy,
I'm eleven years old and in the fifth grade. My four-year-old brother is mentally retarded and acts like a little baby. I love him very much and spend a lot of time with him. But sometimes I feel embarrassed about bringing my friends to the house because of him. My parents don't know how I feel and I know they wouldn't understand if they knew. Can you help me?

Upset

Dear Upset,
Don't feel guilty about your feelings. It's natural to feel embarrassed about your brother and still love him very much. You'll probably find that if you talk to your parents, they'll understand your mixed feelings. Sometimes people are afraid of something they haven't experienced before or don't know about. You and your friends can learn more about people with disabilities. Also, give your friends a chance to get to know your brother. If your friends are true friends, they'll accept him and you'll feel more comfortable about your family situation. Thanks for writing.

Tracy

Dear Tracy,
I just moved to a new town and would really like to make some friends here. My mom thought I should join a Girl Scout troop, so I did. The other girls seem to be having a lot of fun doing things like putting on skits or playing games. When the leader or the girls ask me to join in, I tell them I'd rather watch. That's not true, but I'm shy and I'm afraid I'll say or do something stupid. Can you help me?

Shy

Dear Shy,
After one of your Girl Scout meetings, you might try talking to your troop leader. Tell her you'd like to participate more, but don't feel very comfortable. She'll probably have some ideas that will help you fit in. You can also try to develop a friendship with a girl in your troop who seems to be especially kind. Ask her if you can join in an activity that she's doing alone. As you build your confidence, you'll find it easier to join in larger and larger groups. Don't expect big changes all at once. Just take one step at a time.

Tracy

Your Body

The human body is like a machine in that its parts—bones, muscles, joints, organs, and fat—all work together. Every person's body looks a little different. You may not always like the way you look. For example, you may think you're too heavy or too thin. If so, check with a doctor or nurse to find out what weight is right for you and what you can do to lose or gain weight if necessary.

In general, be happy with your body and do all you can to care for it. It's the only one you will

ever have! Here are some activities to help you learn more about your body.

■■ Discover how the muscles of your face work. Try these exercises. (It's fun to do them with others.)

Frown—Put your fingertips on your forehead, just above your eyebrows. Where are your frowning muscles? Frown and feel your muscles contract. Then let go of the frown and feel the muscles relax.

Smile—Feel your smiling muscles contract, and then feel them relax as you release the smile.

Blink your eyes—How long can you keep your eyes open without blinking automatically?

Wiggle your ears—Not everybody can do this. Can you?

■■ Find out about the areas of your tongue, called taste buds, that are sensitive to salty, sweet, bitter, and sour tastes.

You will need: pieces of food, different kinds of juices and other liquids, clean stick cotton swabs, water.

Crush small pieces of food and touch them to each area of the tongue (shown in the diagram). When testing liquids, use clean cotton swabs to place some of the liquid on your tongue. Where is each taste sensation strongest? For example, does a piece of apple seem sweeter when touched to the

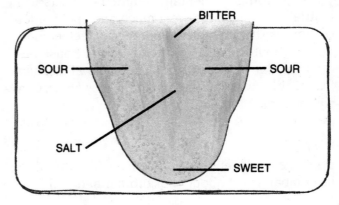

tip, side, or back of the tongue? Use water to rinse your mouth after each test.

■■ In this activity, find out how your sense of taste is affected by your sense of smell.

You will need: a blindfold, pieces of foods like apple, banana, macaroni, cheese, ketchup, mustard, raw potato, raw onion.

Put on the blindfold. Then pinch your nostrils closed with your fingertips. After two to three minutes of breathing through your mouth—not your nose—have a helper place a piece of food in your mouth. Try to guess what it is by using only the sense of taste. (Be sure not to swallow the food until you let go of your nostrils.) Rinse your mouth with water and try some other foods. You may be surprised by the results!

■■ Measure your pulse rate. Take your pulse by placing your index and middle fingers on the inside of your wrist. Count how many beats you feel for 10 seconds, and multiply that number by 6 to get your pulse rate for one minute.

Record your pulse rate here: _____ .

Run in place for 30 seconds and take your pulse again.

Record the rate here: _____ .

After resting for 5 minutes, take your pulse again.

What is it now? _____

■■ Help your body relax. Sit or lie down in a comfortable position. Close your eyes and relax. Now you are going to relax your body parts, one part at a time. Picture in your mind each body part as you relax it. Relax your cheeks, your mouth, your head. Relax your shoulders, arms, and hands. Now relax your chest and stomach. Relax your hips and then your legs. Picture your thighs and calves going limp. Now, relax your feet and toes. Your whole body should feel relaxed now. Stay relaxed for a couple of minutes. . . . Count from 1 to 10, slowly waking your body. At the count of 10, open your eyes.

Another way to do this relaxation exercise is to have someone read the above ideas to you. Get a partner, and take turns helping each other to relax.

DID YOU KNOW?

There are over 600 muscles in the human body.
It takes 43 muscles to frown.
It takes only 17 muscles to smile.
The largest muscle is the gluteus maximus—it's the muscle you sit on.

WHAT IS PUBERTY?

Between roughly the ages of 8 and 16, many changes occur in the body that give you a more adult appearance. This period of change is called puberty. Every girl has her own rate of growth and of changes at puberty. In any group of girls, there will be different rates of change—some girls will change quickly, other girls more slowly. Sometimes a girl may feel embarrassed or concerned about how her body is changing. These feelings are normal—the whole body is changing, and that includes thoughts and feelings.

One of the most important changes in your body will be the start of menstruation, which is the monthly flow of blood tissue from the uterus. Girls usually begin menstruating between ages 9 and 16. You may have heard menstruation called "a period." That's because it happens periodically about every 28 days—and usually lasts for three to seven days. (In the beginning it may be more irregular, though.) Learn as much as you can about menstruation by talking with an adult you trust, such as a parent, teacher, school nurse, Girl Scout leader, or adult friend. Menstruation is a healthy function of the female body and nothing to be worried about or ashamed of. It means you are maturing and becoming a young woman.

■ Keep a diary or notebook of the bodily changes you notice and the feelings you have about those changes. Keep this diary in a private place for your use only, and add to it from time to time.

■ Talk to the women in your family about how they grew when they were your age. For example, ask them when they reached their full height and how they felt about the rapid changes during puberty.

■ Read the "Day by Day—Skills for Living" chapter on pages 85–118 to find out more about how to take care of your body.

HOW PHYSICALLY FIT ARE YOU?

Whether you are walking, sleeping, playing baseball, or watching television, your body is working and using energy. Good physical fitness can help your body run smoothly and function at its very best. Being fit helps to improve both your health and your appearance.

An important part of fitness is using your muscles to keep them active and strong. There are many muscles you use every day without even thinking about it. For example:

- Arm muscles—Help you raise your arm to answer a question in class, or bend your elbow to throw a ball
- Leg muscles—Help you run, stand, and climb a hill
- Diaphragm muscle—Helps you breathe, sneeze, and talk
- Back muscles—Help you stand up; also help you to maintain good posture.

Can you name some other muscles you use during the day?

Exercising regularly is an important way of becoming physically fit. Exercise helps you to develop flexibility, strength, and endurance.

- **Flexibility** is the ability to move your joints in different directions.
- **Strength** is the ability to use your muscles with force.
- **Endurance** is the ability to do something for a long time without getting tired.

Here are some ways to measure your flexibility, strength, and endurance.

Measure Your Flexibility

■ After doing some warm-up exercises (described on pages 38–40), try a flexibility exercise.

Sit-and-reach test Measure a distance of 12 inches (30 centimeters)* away from a wall. Mark the spot with a strip of tape. Remove your shoes. Facing the wall, sit on the floor with your legs extended in front of you. Place the heels of your feet on top of the tape. With one hand on top of the other, slowly reach forward. Keep your hands together. How far do you reach? The closer you get to the wall, the more flexible you are.

Chest lifts Lie on your stomach with your hands clasped behind your neck. Slowly raise your chin and chest off the floor. Have someone help you

*The metric equivalents given in this handbook are approximate.

measure the distance from your chin to the floor. The greater the distance, the more flexible you are.

Measure Your Strength

■ Do some warm-up exercises before trying to test your strength.

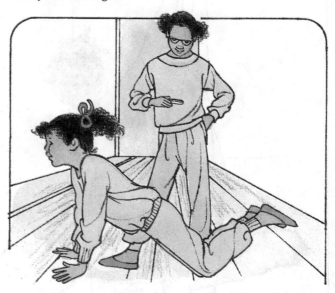

Push-ups Lie face down with your hands on the ground outside your shoulders, fingers pointing forward, knees bent. Lift your body by straightening your arms, keeping your back straight. Return to the starting position and repeat. Have your friend time you for 30 seconds. How many push-ups did you do?

Wall jump Stand facing a wall. Raise both arms over your head and reach as high as you can on your tiptoes. Have your friend mark the spot where you touch the wall.

Now, squat down and jump as high as you can and touch the wall. Mark this spot and measure the distance between the two marks.

Measure Your Endurance

■ Remember to do some warm-up exercises before trying one of these activities.

Jumping rope Jump until you get tired. How much time did you spend jumping?

Jogging/walking Pick a measured area like a school track or jogging trail. See how far you can jog in 10 minutes. Walk for a while if you get tired, then jog again. Measure how far you were able to go. Take measurements at different times, and keep a record of your progress.

Once you have started a regular exercise program, you can repeat these tests every few weeks to keep track of your progress. Make a chart on which you can record your later results so that they can be compared with your earlier results.

EXERCISES FOR GREATER FITNESS

The warm-up, work-out, and cool-down are the three important parts of an exercise routine.

Warm-up Exercises

■ To keep your muscles from becoming stiff, sore, or injured, it is important to do warm-up exercises before taking part in a fitness or sports activity. Work up to doing each one several times. Try some of these:

Windmills Hold your arms straight out to your sides. Twirl them around 8 times one way and 8 times the other. Feel the working of the muscles in your arms and shoulders.

Back stretch Stand straight with your feet about 12 inches (30 cm) apart and your arms down. While breathing out, slowly bend over, keeping your knees slightly bent, and touch the floor between your feet (or as far down as you can bend). Hold this position for 10 to 15 seconds. Then return to the starting position while breathing in deeply. This exercise stretches both the upper back and the backs of the thighs near the knee. Rest for 10 seconds; then bend again.

Side stretch Stand with your feet about 12 inches (30 cm) apart. Lean to your right side, reaching down with your right arm. Reach over your head with your left arm. Feel the gentle stretching of your arm and side muscles. Hold the position for 10 seconds. Repeat on the other side.

Calf stretcher Stand facing a wall at arm's-length distance, with your hands flat against the wall. Keeping your legs straight, lean forward by bending your arms. Keep your feet on the ground with your

toes turned slightly inward. Feel the muscles in the backs of your legs being stretched.

One-leg hug   Lie on your back. Lift up one knee and pull it to your chest with both arms. Keep the other leg straight and flat on the ground. Curl your head and shoulders toward your knee. Now, do this with the other leg.

Side leg raise   Lie on the ground on your side. Lift your top leg up. Try to keep your leg straight and in a direct line with your body as it is lifted. Now, lie on your other side and repeat this exercise with the other leg.

If you haven't been exercising your muscles, you may feel a little sore. Don't overdo it. Work at your own pace.

The Work-Out

■   The work-out part of a routine includes more vigorous exercises that are done for longer periods of time. They help to strengthen your heart and lungs. Bicycling, swimming, walking, jogging, skating, and aerobic dance can give you a good work-out. You can do them alone, or with a friend or family member. Make sure your muscles are warmed up before you start. A good work-out should last about 20 minutes.

Aerobic Dance   Aerobic dancing involves moving continuously to music and doing dance steps. Jumping, kicking, jogging, stretching, sliding, and swinging are all aerobic dance movements.

For aerobic dancing you will need to wear comfortable clothing. Leotards or shorts and tights are best. Make sure you wear sturdy gym sneakers.

Before you start dancing, take your resting pulse rate to find out how fast your heart is beating. See page 35 for instructions on how to take your pulse.

While exercising, you will want to reach your target heart rate. To figure out what this should be, subtract your age from 220, then multiply the answer by 70 percent. For example:

```
  220                210
− 10 (your age)    ×  .70
  210               147.00  = your target heart rate
```

Record your resting pulse rate here: _____

Record your target heart rate here: _____

Now that you're ready to begin, put on your favorite music. Here are some steps you could try:

- Jog in place slowly, then pick up speed.
- Kick one leg out in front of you. Clap your hands under your leg as you kick. Then do the same on the other side.
- Kick one leg out to the side, then the other.
- Kick your right leg behind you, then your left leg.
- Jump up and down.
- Hop on one foot, then the other.
- Twist your waist from side to side as you jump.
- Walk while swinging your arms back and forth.
- Slide to the right and then to the left.
- You can also make up steps of your own.

Dance for 10 minutes. Take your pulse rate as soon as you are finished. Are you exercising so that you reach nearly your target heart rate? If so, you're doing fine. If the rate is *higher* than the target, you need to slow down.

Now do aerobic dancing for 10 more minutes. Take your pulse again.

Cool-Down

■   Right after vigorous exercise, you should cool down. A cool-down period is needed to relax your muscles and let your body return to normal. Walking, slow jogging, and stretching exercises are good for cool-downs. They should be done for at least 5 minutes.

Yoga   Yoga exercises, which are thousands of years old, are a good way of cooling down. The people of India developed them by looking at the movements of animals and birds—like the movement of a swan stretching its long neck. Here are two yoga exercises to try.

THE FISH

1. Lie down on your back with your legs stretched out and your arms at your sides. Curl your fingers.

2. Stiffen your legs by pointing your toes. Make fists with your hands.

3. Inhale (breathe in) through your nose. Raise yourself up on your elbows. Gently arch your back by pushing your chest up and tilting your head back.

4. Hold that arched position for about 5 seconds.

5. Exhale (breathe out). Slowly return to your beginning position by sliding your head back. Relax your legs, arms, and hands.

Slowly work up to doing The Fish three times in a row.

THE CAT

1. Get down on your hands and knees.

2. Arch your back slowly. Bring your head down. Tighten your stomach muscles.

3. Continue arching. Get your chin as close to your chest as possible. Tighten your buttock muscles. Count to 5.

4. Slowly push your back down and push your head and buttocks up. Tighten your buttock muscles.

5. Raise your face to the ceiling. Hold for 5 seconds. Relax. Repeat once.

Your Own Fitness Routine

■ You can make up your own routine for keeping fit. Be sure to include a warm-up, work-out, and cool-down. Record your routine here. Do this routine 3 times a week for one month. How do you feel at the end of that month?

MY FITNESS ROUTINE

Warm-Up
(10 minutes) _____

Work-Out
(20-30 minutes) _____

Cool-Down
(5 minutes) _____

Who Am I?

■ Now that you've done some activities and had a chance to think about your interests, values, bodily changes, talents, hobbies, and feelings, answer the question "Who am I?" in 10 different ways.

I am _____ .

I am _____ .

I am _____.   I am _____.

I am _____.   I am _____.

I am _____.   I am _____.

I am _____.   I am _____.

CHAPTER 3

Relationships

Everyone's world is filled with people—and as you get older, you'll get to know more and more of them. There are some people you'll only meet once or twice. Other people will play very important parts in your life.

■■ You relate to different people in different ways. Think about the characteristics of people listed below. Do these characteristics affect how you treat others or how they treat you?

- Age. Do you treat people who are younger than you differently from the way you treat those who are older?
- Sex. Do your relationships with girls differ from those with boys?
- Occupation. Do you relate to your teacher in the same way that you relate to the person who delivers your mail?
- How well you know the person. When someone meets you for the first time, does she treat you the same way that an old friend treats you?

- Appearance. Do you treat someone who you think is good-looking differently from the way you treat someone who you think isn't good-looking?

Sometimes it's unfair to treat people differently because of a characteristic they have. Girl Scouts learn that treating someone differently because she is of another race or religion is unjust and goes against the Girl Scout Promise and Law.

However, in other instances, it makes sense to treat people in different ways. If you talked to a two-year-old the way you talk to your friends, that young child might have trouble understanding what you mean.

Building Relationships

Each relationship is unique—but all relationships involve sharing, talking, and spending time together.

Some relationships are very happy, while others are not in such good shape. If a relationship has problems, it is usually worth working to improve it. And even relationships that are already good can get better. Here are some ways of building better relationships with others.

SHARING AND LISTENING

Spending time with someone—playing games, going on trips, or just talking—is an important part of a good relationship. Sharing your thoughts and feelings is a good way to develop closeness. So is listening to others. What does Janice really mean? Why is Martina saying that? How would I feel if I were in that situation? Hopefully, the other person will be listening to and understanding you in the same way.

DISCUSSING AND DISAGREEING

One way to improve a relationship is to talk about problems in that relationship. Usually it's best to discuss things as they come up. Waiting to talk about something until you're ready to explode will only result in a loud explosion!

It's normal for people to disagree at times. It can even be helpful to argue, if the argument results in a greater understanding of each other. If you do argue, though, keep the following in mind:

- Always try to be fair and honest.
- Be specific. Focus on what's bothering you, and don't bring up unrelated subjects.
- Don't call names. Calling someone "stupid" or a "jerk" will not help you make your point. And name-calling can hurt another person so much that it may be the only part of the argument remembered.
- Be calm. Try to stay in control. You'll be more likely to say what you mean that way. (Hint: Count to ten before speaking.)
- Listen. Discussion involves two people, not just yourself. Listen carefully to the other person.
- Don't let a disagreement destroy the relationship. Maybe neither of you will change your mind. You may have to agree to disagree—and when the argument is over, it's over!

ROLE-PLAYING

Relationships can also be strengthened by role-playing. By acting out a particular role, you will understand better how someone in another position might feel.

■ ■ ■ Here are some stories that can be role-played with others:

- A family has an argument about vacation plans.
- Five friends try to decide what to do after school.
- A girl is wrongly blamed for cheating in school.
- A new girl joins your Girl Scout troop.

In groups of three to five girls, pick one of the above situations to role-play before the troop. Or, make up your own situation to role-play. Work out a satisfactory solution, decision, or other ending to the situation.

Knowing People Better

■■■ Show that you are really interested in learning more about others by doing some of the following activities:

- Write to or call someone you haven't seen or heard from in a long time.
- Make a young child laugh.
- Say something nice (and mean it) to someone you live with.
- Run an errand for an elderly person.
- Teach a skill that you have to a friend.
- When someone tells you she has a problem, listen to her carefully and, if you can, try to help.
- Make a gift for someone in your family.
- Spend some time with someone who seems to be lonely.

Remember the Girl Scout Law. If you show respect for yourself and others and do your best to be honest and fair, helpful and considerate, cheerful and friendly, your relationships with others can only get better!

Family

Families come in different sizes and forms. Most often, the term "family" refers to close relatives such as mother, father, sister, and brother. The term may also refer to other important people who care for and support you. You may live with two parents or with one, or you may be cared for and loved by people who are not your parents. Great-grandparents, grandparents, stepparents, foster parents, guardians, aunts, uncles, and cousins may be part of your family. They may live with you, nearby, or far away. You may see them frequently or only on special occasions.

What makes a family special? A family can give its members things they need like love, security, food, clothing, shelter, safety, and a sense of being important.

WHO IS IN YOUR FAMILY?

■■ Draw pictures or paste photographs of yourself and the members of your family on a piece of construction paper to make a family collage. Label family members by name, relationship, and whether they live with you, nearby, or far away. Don't forget your pets—they can be an important part of your family.

■■ Share stories about your pets or various family members with the girls in your troop or group.

■■ Write a paragraph about what makes your family special to you. Share this information with the members of your family. Ask each member what she or he finds special about the family.

ENJOYING FAMILY ACTIVITIES

Take a moment to think about the activities that your family most enjoys. These may be activities that everyone does together, or ones that only a few family members do. Some examples are going on a picnic, decorating the house for a holiday, camping out, going bicycle riding together.

■■ Plan an activity to do with your family.

SHARING FAMILY FEELINGS

The way your family members express their feelings is very personal. In each family, there are different ways of showing love, concern, togetherness, happiness, anger, or frustration. Talking or touching, or both, can be important in a family.

RESPONSIBILITIES AS A FAMILY MEMBER

■■■ Fill in the chart below to show the responsibilities that you and other members of your family have in your household. Check the jobs that each person does. In the extra space on the chart, add chores that are not already listed.

		FAMILY MEMBERS			
DISHES	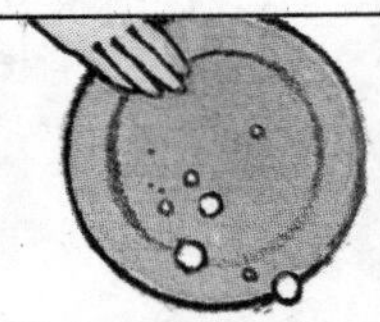				
SHOPS					
COOKS					
FIXES THINGS	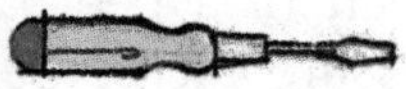				
LAUNDRY	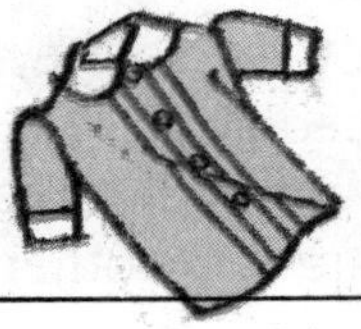				

Peers

Peers are people who are your age or who are your equal in other ways—for example, they may be equal to you in ability. Peers include the girls in your troop, your other friends, your classmates, and even girls and boys your age whom you've never met. As you grow older, your circle of peers will grow even wider and you will become a part of many different peer groups.

Some good things about being a member of a peer group are that you:

- Can do activities with people with whom you have a lot in common.
- Can often get more done as a group member than you could alone.
- Feel that you're not alone—that you belong to a group.
- Can share your talents and skills with others.
- Can learn from what your peers have experienced in their lives.
- Can find out more about yourself and who you are.

PEER PRESSURE

One problem with being part of a peer group is that peers may start to pressure each other to act a certain way, to look a certain way, or to have only certain individuals as friends.

Some people pressure others so they can feel "better" than others. Other people feel they will be more popular if they can be a leader or get others to do what they want. What are some other reasons that people may pressure others?

What can you do when faced with peer pressure? Some ideas that have worked for others are:

- Be yourself! Be proud of who you are. Try not to let others lead you to do something you would be ashamed of later. Most people respect others who have the courage to act the way they believe is right.
- Communicate! Tell people how you feel. Maybe others will learn something from you if you tell them what you think about the issue at hand.
- Respect the feelings and decisions of others.

After you have expressed yourself, let others follow their own decisions and you follow yours.

- If necessary, find support elsewhere. Sometimes, if people keep pressuring you, the best thing to do is stay away from them or ignore them. Find other people who feel the same way you do.

ADVICE FROM PEERS

Often, people consider the feelings and opinions of their peers when trying to make a decision. Sometimes the information you receive from others is helpful, and sometimes it is not.

ACTIVITIES INVOLVING PEERS

■ ■ PASS A PEER A COMPLIMENT Get a group of your peers together. Sit in a circle with one person in the center who will receive the compliments. Each person takes a turn and gives an honest compliment to the person in the center, who listens without saying anything. After everyone has given a compliment to the person in the center, she returns to the circle and the person on her left goes into the center. The game continues until everyone has had a chance to be in the center.

■ ■ ■ PERFORM A PEER PLAY Get a group of peers together and discuss, write, practice, and perform a play about peer pressure. Pick an issue that you feel is faced by many girls where you live. For example, the play might be about being pressured to smoke or try drugs. Invite parents and friends to see the play.

■ ■ WRITE A PEER PACT Try working with some peers to develop a pact, which is an agreement among people. If a peer pact is based on important values, it can be a positive example of peer pressure that works to benefit everyone.

When you became a Girl Scout, you made a promise to try to live by the things you said in the Girl Scout Promise and Law. The other girls in your troop promised also to try to do this. So, a peer pact already exists among you! Try putting the pact to work:

- Get a group of your peers together.
- Choose a part of the Girl Scout Law that you would like to work on as a group.
- Write a pact together that describes some-

thing your peer group will do to carry out that part of the Law. Include a deadline for each task involved.

- Have everyone in the group sign the pact.
- Have fun making your peer pact come alive!

Friends

A friend is an important person, a special kind of peer. Friends:

- care about each other
- are there for each other
- can be trusted
- can keep secrets
- believe in each other
- respect each other's ideas and values
- are fun to be with!

WHAT FRIENDSHIP MEANS

■ ■ What is it about a person that makes you want to be her or his friend? Start by thinking about yourself and the way you like others to treat you. Then complete the following sentences:

- I enjoy _____ with my friends.

- I'm unhappy when my friends _____

- I'm proud that my friends _____

- I listen to my friends when _____

- I wish my friends _____

■ ■ Now find out how other people feel about the meaning of friendship. Ask ten different people (of different ages and backgrounds) to give you five words that describe a friend. What ideas are mentioned by a lot of people? What ideas are different from person to person? Which words were used most often?

WHAT ARE YOUR FRIENDS LIKE?

Think about the people who are your friends now. You already know and like something about each of them, but you don't know everything about your friends. By being a good observer and reporter, you can learn more about old friends and may even make new friends.

■■■ You might want to make a "My Friends" scrapbook. Here are some things you could list about your friends and your friendships:

- Full name
- Nickname
- Age
- Favorite dessert, movie, color, food, sport, singing group, actor/actress, games
- Hobbies
- People and pets in her/his family
- Where and when we met
- What I like best about her/him
- What we like to do together

You can make a new scrapbook each year as your friendships or friends change.

DIFFERENT KINDS OF FRIENDS

With each of your friends, you have a different kind of relationship. You may not do and talk about the same things with all of your friends. So, people who are your friends may see you and know you in different ways.

How comfortable are you with different friends? What things about yourself do you share with them? What do you look for in a friendship?

■■ Look over the list below. For each statement, write down the name of a friend who comes to mind. Add your own statements in the blank spaces, along with a friend's name for each one.

Are there many different names? Do you think the names might change six months from now? a year from now? Redo the list from time to time. Are there any changes? Make sure you mark the date each time you write up a new list.

BEING A FRIEND

■■ There are different levels of friendship. The friendships you have with others depend a lot on

A friend is someone I might...	The name of this friend is...
1. Help	1. _____
2. Play with after school	2. _____
3. Ask for advice about a problem I'm having	3. _____
4. Invite to my house	4. _____
5. Tell a big secret to	5. _____
6. Tell about my family	6. _____
7. Sit with at lunch	7. _____
8. _____	8. _____
9. _____	9. _____
10. _____	10. _____

you. Let's see how this works. Think about some-one whom you consider a friend. Keep this person in mind as you answer "yes" or "no" to each question below.

What Kind of Friend Am I?

		YES	NO
1.	I listen carefully to my friend when she talks about something important to her.	___	___
2.	I might be upset with my friend, but I still speak to her.	___	___
3.	It doesn't bother me if my friend sometimes has other things to do.	___	___
4.	I let my friend know what I like about her.	___	___
5.	Sometimes my friend decides how we're going to spend our time.	___	___
6.	I share secrets with my friend.	___	___
7.	My friend and I like to do things together.	___	___
8.	I do not try to make my friend be just like me.	___	___

Find out what your score means. Count the number of times you said "yes." If your score is

7 or 8	—You are a super friend!
5 or 6	—You are a very good friend.
4	—You are a nice friend—sometimes!
3 or below	—You are an acquaintance. Maybe you need to try harder.

PEN PALS—A FRIENDSHIP BY MAIL

A pen pal is a friend you get acquainted with through letters. She usually lives in another state or country, and will write about her hometown, school, family, customs and traditions, and special interests. Pen pals share things like games, recipes, solutions to problems, and snapshots. For more information about pen pals from other countries, see page 82.

Adults

Although you spend a great deal of time with people your own age, many adults are also part of your life. Your life is certainly affected by the adults around you—family members, teachers in school, your Girl Scout leader. You may come in contact with some adults who understand you, and with others who do not know what you really mean or how you feel. You may have a great time with some adults and not get along with others.

■■ Who are the most important adults in your life? Write down their names and then give reasons why they are important.

Many adults are in powerful positions, and you may feel you cannot influence their decisions. However, you don't have to wait until you're an adult to take an active part in what is going on

around you. Writing can be one way to let adults know something about you.

■■ Write a letter to . . .
- an adult friend or relative
- your representative in Congress
- your senator
- the staff of your Girl Scout council
- an official in your local government, such as the mayor
- a company president

to express your . . .
- concern
- opinion
- appreciation
- ideas

Keep track of the responses you receive.

Groups

There are many types of groups, and you may act very differently in each one. It is possible to be a leader in one group, but not in another. You might be shy in one group, but outgoing with a different group.

Sometimes one individual becomes a scapegoat in a group. That is, she gets picked on and blamed for everything that goes wrong, even when it's not her fault. If someone in your group has become a scapegoat, try to do something to stop it. Making someone a scapegoat is unfair and hurts the person's feelings.

YOUR GROUPS

■■ Leaders, followers, active participants, people who joke around—all are important members of groups. List the groups that you are part of and describe how you act in each one.

WHAT HAPPENS IN A GROUP?

When you're part of a group, do you act differently from the way you do when you're alone? People sometimes take greater risks when they're with others. They do things that they wouldn't do on their own. Read about the experiences of Lotus and Gloria.

LOTUS

Lotus was walking slowly to school one beautiful sunny morning at the end of May, when Kristen, Rita, and Josie caught up with her. "How about going with us to the lake today?" asked Kristen. "But we can't do that—it's a school day," Lotus protested. "Oh yes we can. School is so boring and it's a great day for swimming," answered Josie. Before Lotus had a chance to protest again, Rita said, "Come on, we're all going. It'll be fun." "Well . . . OK, I'll come," Lotus decided.

Has something like that ever happened to you? What did you do?

Groups can sometimes be very helpful. A group may encourage you to do something that you want to do but have been afraid to try. Here's what happened to Gloria.

GLORIA, STAR OF THE TEAM

Gloria had always loved softball. Ever since she was in kindergarten she had played the game with her friends and sometimes with members of her family. She wanted to try out for her school softball

team, but was scared by the idea of everyone watching her at the tryouts. Then, two of Gloria's friends decided to try out for the team. This was just the push Gloria needed—she felt much less nervous about trying out when she realized she'd be doing it with two friends. Gloria was chosen for the team, and ended up becoming one of the best players.

Can you remember a time when being part of a group helped you to achieve something?

FUN IN GROUPS

■ ■ In a group, you often have the chance to do things that you couldn't do alone. Meet with your troop, or with some other group of friends, and think up as many activities as possible for having fun in groups. Below are a few examples to get you started:

- Putting on a play
- Making popcorn
- Running relay races
- Camping out
- Having a party

After brainstorming for a while, you'll have plenty of ideas for future group activities.

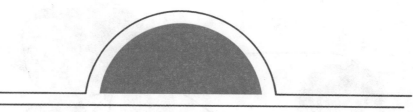

CHAPTER 4

Decisions, Decisions, Decisions

Which brand of jeans should I buy? Should I tell my friend Rona that I'm angry with her? Which book should I borrow from the library? How much time should I spend today working on my Sports Sampler badge? How do I tell the teacher about the cheating in the science lab? What can I do about my shyness? Should I play with Juana or Michelle after school? How do I let Rafael know that I like him?

These kinds of questions don't have a single answer. They're different from the questions your teacher might ask when you're in your math class. When she asks how much is 8 multiplied by 4, you know that the correct answer is 32. But questions like the ones above require *decisions*—choices must be made between two or more possibilities. And there will not always be one right answer.

This chapter is about decision-making. It is about choices that you are making right now, every day. The chapter is also about the kind of decision-making you will be working at more and more as

you grow older. For instance, have you begun to think about where you want to live when you're grown up? about the kind of work you'd like to do when you're an adult? about whether or not you want to get married someday? It's certainly too soon to make any final decisions on those subjects. But it's a good idea to start thinking about how decisions get made and to start practicing. Then you'll be ready for those big decisions that come later.

You're Already a Decision-Maker!

Sometimes, it may seem that decisions are made only by adults. But, in fact, everyone makes decisions every day about a great variety of things. Often you make a decision without even being aware that you've done so. When you selected your clothes this morning, were you really aware that you were making a decision? When you brushed your teeth, were you aware that you had decided to do that?

Two Hours in the Life of a Decision-Maker

This activity can help you to see yourself as the decision-maker you are. On the chart below, keep a record of all the decisions you make in a two-hour period. You can start this activity at any time.

An example is shown to help you complete the chart. Try to include all decisions, even those that seem unimportant.

Date _____

Time you begin _____

Time you end _____

The general situation	The decision	How long the decision took	Person(s) who influenced you in making the decision
Example			
Selecting clothes for school	I picked a red blouse and blue pants	2 minutes	My sister
_____	_____	_____	_____
_____	_____	_____	_____
_____	_____	_____	_____
_____	_____	_____	_____
_____	_____	_____	_____
_____	_____	_____	_____
_____	_____	_____	_____
_____	_____	_____	_____
_____	_____	_____	_____
_____	_____	_____	_____
_____	_____	_____	_____
_____	_____	_____	_____

What did you find out about yourself by keeping this chart?

- How quickly do you make most of your decisions?
- Who most often helps you to make them?
- Did you make more or fewer decisions than you expected?
- How long does it usually take you to make decisions?

Troop members or other friends might find it interesting to compare their decision charts.

You can repeat this activity many times. Just make a new chart for yourself whenever you try it again. You'll learn something different about yourself each time.

Should I? Shouldn't I? Should I? Shouldn't I?

Some people seem to have an easy time making decisions. When Jennifer is asked by her friends whether she wants to go see a comedy film or the new science fiction movie, she thinks for just a moment and then makes up her mind.

On the other hand, when Doreen is asked the question, she goes through all the reasons why she might want to see the comedy film. Then she thinks of all the reasons for seeing the science fiction picture. Then she goes through both lists again in case she forgot a reason.

By the time Doreen is ready to make a decision and to offer an opinion, her friends are already on the way downtown to the film of their choice. Because Doreen took so long, her friends went ahead and made the decision without her. That's what happens sometimes when you can't make up your mind.

Are you more like Jennifer or Doreen?

Why Should You Be a Decision-Maker?

Active decision-making gives you more power, more control over your life, and greater confidence in yourself. Sally, as you will see below, is a girl who doesn't take advantage of decision-making opportunities.

SALLY DOESN'T DECIDE

On Tuesday morning, eleven-year-old Sally Greene woke up late. Her mother hadn't called to wake her until eight o'clock. Sally should have been up by 7:30 at the latest. Practically all she had time to do was brush her teeth and throw on the clothes her mother had picked out for her. She didn't have time to eat breakfast or to pick out an outfit on her own. She just wore the blouse that her mother loved and that she hated because the style was so old-fashioned. She rushed off to school hungry and in a terrible mood.

■   Rewrite the story about Sally so that she makes more of the decisions and can leave for school in a better mood.

■■   With your troop, group, or other friends, put on a skit about a girl who lets other people make decisions for her. Then put on a skit about a girl who has learned to make her own decisions.

Other People Sometimes Make the Decisions

Sometimes, other people will make important decisions that affect your life. Read about what happened to Keiko.

A DECISION BY KEIKO'S PARENTS

When Keiko came down to breakfast Sunday morning, her father said that there was something important he needed to tell her. "We have to move

to another town," he said. "I've been transferred to the company's Michigan office and we're going to have to sell this house and find a new place to live by the end of the summer." Keiko's mother explained that the move was "absolutely necessary" and that they would have about a month to get ready. Keiko couldn't believe what she had just heard. All she could think about was that she'd be leaving her best friend Linda and that she wouldn't be able to graduate from Abraham Lincoln Elementary School next June with all her friends. Keiko had been expecting to be in Ms. Rosen's sixth-grade class in September, and everyone knew that she was the best teacher in the school. Now Keiko was moving. It wasn't her decision to go to Michigan, but she knew there wasn't anything she could do about it.

In this story, Keiko's parents made a decision that would have a great effect on her life. Events outside of our control often happen, even to adults, and sometimes they make people feel unhappy and helpless.

But even when an important decision, like moving away, is made by someone else, there are many other decisions that you can still make. For example, Keiko can decide whether she's going to have a going-away party, whether she'll write to her old friends, and how she'll make new friends in Michigan.

■ Write about a time when someone else made an important decision that affected you. Were you able to play any part in the decision-making?

After writing the experience down, share it with other girls in your group or troop. Listen to their stories. Do you think you or the others could have influenced the decisions that were made?

■ One of the nicest parts of growing up is that you will have more and more opportunities to make important decisions. Write about a time when you made an important decision. Review what you have written, and then share the story with other girls in your group or troop. Discuss how each of you felt after the decision was made.

Deciding to Decide

Sometimes, it's so easy to let other people make decisons for you. But when others make all the decisions, you may not get the chance to do what you really want. Deciding that you're going to make more decisions is an important step in becoming a leader. Find out more about leadership in the next chapter.

Steps to a Decision

Once you've decided you're going to be a more active decision-maker, how do you actually make those decisions? There are steps you can take to help you in making decisions. You don't go through all these steps for every decision, but it's important to keep them in mind for *big* decisions. Here's how Rosita went through the steps in the decision-making process.

ROSITA'S DECISION

It's the first day of sixth grade. Each student has been asked to decide on the one special after-school activity she will become involved in. The list of choices is a long one: They range from piano lessons to volleyball, and from modern dance to painting. Rosita has to give the answer to her teacher by the end of the day.

Step 1: Know the Problem or Issue
Rosita needs to decide which activity she will become involved in. If she doesn't make her own decision, the decision will be made for her by her

want to get into better physical shape? Rosita may also need to think about some practical matters related to the different activities. For instance, piano lessons are given only on Monday afternoons, but that's when the aerobic dance club meets.

Step 3: Think of All the Ways the Problem Could Be Solved

At this point, Rosita can try to come up with as many ways as possible for solving the problem. Below are a couple of possibilities:

1. She could choose to take piano lessons as her after-school activity and try to get into shape through Girl Scout activities.

2. She could convince her friends to join the volleyball team. Then she could get physical exercise and be with her friends at the same time.

It is important to freely develop ideas without criticizing them right away. A solution that seems foolish at first may become the idea that works best.

Step 4: Look at the Good and Bad Points of Each Idea

Look at each idea and see how well it fits in with your needs, your values, and your interests. For instance, Rosita might realize that her friends don't really like volleyball.

When exploring different possibilities, Rosita might make a list like the one below to help her.

teacher. The real issue is: What does Rosita want to gain from this special after-school experience?

Step 2: Collect Information About Yourself and the Situation

Rosita needs to examine her values, talents, and interests. For example, is spending extra time with friends more important than learning how to play the piano? She should also think about her goals. Does she want to start a new hobby? Does she

	Good Points	Bad Points
Solution 1: _____	_____	_____
Solution 2: _____	_____	_____
Solution 3: _____	_____	_____
Solution 4: _____	_____	_____
Solution 5: _____	_____	_____
Solution 6: _____	_____	_____
Solution 7: _____	_____	_____

Step 5: Make a Decision

After looking at all the information, it is finally time to make a decision, to find the best solution for you. Rosita decides to choose piano lessons as her special after-school activity and to work on her other goals of physical fitness and being with friends through Girl Scout activities.

Step 6: Take Action

Now that the decision has been made, the next step involves taking action Rosita tells her teacher that she has made up her mind and she signs up for piano lessons. Rosita also talks to her Girl Scout troop leader about her interest in physical fitness. At the leader's suggestion, Rosita and some of the other troop members decide to work on the Hiker badge.

Step 7: See If You're Happy with the Results of Your Decision

You may think that once the decision has been made, your work is over. But the decision may need to be looked at again. The choice may have seemed and been right at the time. But you may realize later that a new decision needs to be made.

For three months, Rosita loved taking the piano lessons. But then her piano teacher was transferred to another school, and the new teacher was very good at flute lessons but wasn't a very good piano teacher. Rosita was becoming discouraged. Music was no longer fun for her.

Rosita decided she needed to do some thinking. Things had changed so much since she had made the decision to take piano lessons. It seemed to be time for a new decision.

PRACTICE MAKING A DECISION

■ Now it's your turn to work through the steps of decision-making. Make a decision about your schoolwork, a Girl Scout activity, your family life, or any other subject of your choice. Then carry out the decision.

What was your decision?

_____

_____

What happened after you made the decision?

_____

_____

How do you feel about the decision you made?

_____

_____

Who Helps You Make Decisions?

RENEE'S NEW DRESS

Barbara is getting married in two months, and her 13-year-old sister Renee is very excited about it. The family is already busy making plans about the food, the flowers, the ceremony, and the music.

This afternoon Renee is going shopping to find a dress to wear to the wedding. It's important to her that the dress be very special, because Renee wants Barbara to be proud of her. Although Renee usually shops for clothes with her mother or with her friends, she wants her older sister to join her on this shopping trip. Renee feels that Barbara has great taste and can help pick out the perfect dress for the occasion.

Renee wanted her sister's advice because she knew that it would help her make a better decision. In different situations, you might ask for or accept assistance in decision-making from different people. The right person might be a teacher or a parent, a Girl Scout leader or an aunt, an older sister or a younger brother, a best friend or a next-door neighbor. Different people, because they know different kinds of things, may be helpful to you at different times. Also, sometimes you might go to one person rather than another because of embarrassment or fear. You can't expect one person to be helpful in all instances. It's a good idea to get to know many people who can give advice. But remember that not everyone who tries to help you make decisions will have the right answers. You should choose your decision-making "assistants" very carefully.

■ ■ Imagine that you are in the following situations. Who can help you in making these decisions? Think of two or three people for each situation.

Situation	Who will help you decide?	Why?
1. Deciding which television program to watch.		
2. Deciding who will be invited to your birthday party.		
3. Deciding how to tell your best friend why you are angry with her.		
4. Deciding what to be when you grow up.		
5. Deciding who will be your guest at a party given by a friend.		

How Do Others Make Decisions?

Find out how other people make decisions. Is there someone you particularly admire or respect, such as an older sister, a cousin, your Girl Scout leader, or your teacher? Ask her how she makes decisions and whether she might have some decision-making hints for you. Discuss with your friends some good ideas about decision-making that you've gotten from other people.

Making Decisions About Time

Because you will never have enough time to do everything you'd like to, you will always have to make decisions about how to use your time. For instance, this afternoon you might want to do all of these things:

- Work on your book report, which is due early next week
- Go skating with friends
- Watch a favorite television program
- Work on one of your Girl Scout badges
- Listen to your new record album

Is is possible to do all of these things today? Probably not, so you'll have to make some decisions. Here are some activities that can help you decide how to use your time:

■ Make a list of what you need or want to get done. The list could cover one afternoon, an entire day, or even a week. Sometimes, writing down everything you need to do helps you plan your time. Once you have the list written, you can put a star (*) next to those things that are most important. Try to get these done first. As you complete each thing, cross it off the list. You'll feel good when you see how much you've gotten done.

Why not make a "To Do" list for tomorrow? Look at your list during the day to guide your activities. How much did you get done?

■ Figure out your best time for getting things done. You might be an "early day" type of person. That is, you like to get up early in the morning and can start doing things right away. If this seems to describe you, why not do some physical exercises or badge work or letter writing or whatever in the morning?

What if you're a "late day" type of person? That is, you have a hard time getting started in the morning, and sometimes it's a struggle just to get out of bed. For someone like you, it's not a very good idea to wait to finish a school assignment until the morning it's due. You may want to plan to work on your most important projects in the afternoon or evening.

■ Try to plan ahead. If you know you need to do something within two weeks, don't wait until the night before to get started. Even if everything could be arranged in one night (and it probably can't), planning at the last minute doesn't allow any time to take care of problems that may (and probably will) crop up.

■ Keep your interests and goals in mind to guide you as you decide how you're going to use your time. The information in the "Hopes and Dreams" chapter can help you. In the following story, Dara has taken her hopes and dreams into account in making decisions about her time.

DARA'S DREAM

Dara is a 12-year-old Olympic hopeful who has been perfecting her gymnastic abilities since she was six years old. Every day, she spends at least two hours working to improve her skills in this area. For fun, Dara spends some time playing video games a couple of times a week. She knows she'll never be the neighborhood champion in these games, but Dara doesn't feel that she has to be perfect in everything. She has decided that her most important goal is to be excellent at gymnastics. So she spends much more time on that than she does on video games.

Hard Decisions

Some decisions, like figuring out what you're going to have as a snack after school, aren't hard at all. But other decisions are much tougher to make. Sometimes you will be faced with difficult choices. Two are described on the next page, in the stories about Trish and Lisa. Get together with some friends

and read over the stories. Then discuss these questions:

- What different decisions might be made?
- What would *your* decision be? (Have each friend give her own ideas.)
- Why would you choose that decision?
- How would that decision affect you?
- How would that decision affect others?

Do you find that there are a lot of different answers to these questions?

BEING A JUDGE

Trish was very excited about being a judge in the art contest at the county fair. It was a real honor to be chosen for that job. The other judges had narrowed the choice for top prize to two pictures. One was an oil painting of a basket of fruit. Trish recognized it as a work painted by her best friend Mary. It really was quite beautiful and Trish knew that winning first prize would mean a lot to Mary. But Trish felt that another painting, a watercolor of a beach scene, was just a little better than Mary's painting. How should Trish vote?

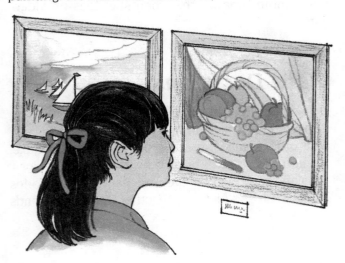

THE SCHOOL TRIP

It had been almost three months since Lisa started saving money for her younger brother's birthday gift. Sammy would be six years old on April 10, which was only two weeks away. Lisa already had a gift in mind that she knew Sammy would love—a remote-control-operated truck. But this morning, Lisa's teacher told her students about a trip to Washington, D.C., that she had arranged for the class during their spring recess. The school would pay some of the expenses, but each student would have to come up with the rest. The amount needed was just about what Lisa had saved for Sammy's birthday gift and she had no other money. Lisa desperately wanted to join her school friends on this trip. What should Lisa do?

■ ■ ■ With your troop or group, make up some other stories about hard decisions. In groups of three to five girls, act out different endings. These decisions can then be discussed by the entire troop.

Decision-Making as a Girl Scout

Girl Scouting gives you many opportunities to develop and use your decision-making skills. While some decisions will be made by you alone, many of them will be made by your group or troop, often with your Girl Scout leader's help. Group decision-making is described in the next chapter.

As you use your handbook, remember that you are a decision-maker!

CHAPTER 5

Leadership and Groups

Everyone has different strengths. Some people are very good at getting along with others. Others are excellent scholars. Some are very skilled athletes. Others do a great job of organizing people and things. Each person has her own talents and special abilities.

Being a Leader

With your special abilities and talents, you will have opportunities throughout your life to be a leader. Being a leader could mean that you are the captain of your team, president of your class in school, a patrol leader in your Junior Girl Scout troop, the head of a club you organized, or the director of a play.

Have you ever been put in charge of a group? If so, write down the leadership positions you have had. Even if you don't have a title (like president or director) that tells others that you head a group, you can still be a leader. You can lead by:

- Helping people to figure out what they want or need to do

- Helping people to carry out plans they have made
- Encouraging people to make suggestions or ask questions
- Trying to get people to be fair and to cooperate with one another

When a group has more than one leader, the leaders should work together for the good of the whole group.

■■ Observe the Patti Simpson Fan Club in action and see if you can pick out the leaders.

THE PATTI SIMPSON FAN CLUB MEETING

The Patti Simpson Fan Club was holding its monthly meeting. Damita, the club's president, called the meeting to order. Lynne suggested that the girls brainstorm to come up with ideas for ways to celebrate singer Patti Simpson's upcoming birthday. Sarah volunteered to record the ideas on the blackboard. As the brainstorming session went on, Denise kept interrupting to criticize the ideas suggested

by others. Melanie, always the peacekeeper, nicely told Denise that she could be more helpful to the group if she followed the rules for brainstorming and gave others a chance to speak openly and freely. The group was then able to get on with its job.

Damita, Lynne, Sarah, and Melanie all took on leadership roles and did things to help their group. From the list below, pick out what they did.

Leaders . . .

plan	show that they
show enthusiasm	accept others
show an understanding	show respect for
of others	others
guide and direct	teach
organize	support
gather information	keep the peace
give information to	keep track of
others	time
recognize problems	take risks
and try to solve	inspire
them	think clearly
are fair-minded	advise
are strong when a	encourage
problem arises	work hard
help others to	show imagination
cooperate	evaluate

EVERYONE CAN BE A LEADER

Given a chance, everyone can be a leader! Because people are talented in different ways, they are leaders at different times and in different situations.

With your group or troop, try this activity that gives everyone the opportunity to be a leader. Each girl chooses an activity or topic that she knows well and prepares a presentation for the group. The group can decide on the amount of time each girl will have to share her special talent or knowledge. Below are some ideas you might consider:

- Camping tips
- Art projects
- Description of a book
- Description of travel to a foreign country
- Exercise or sports techniques (for example, how to stretch before jogging)

How Groups Change

As group members get acquainted with one another, they need to work out ways to get along that will allow them to get things done. Some people are complainers, others suffer in silence. Some people argue, others are disturbed by arguments. This is where real leadership comes in. Leaders can use some of the qualities listed at the left (for example, providing encouragement or showing imagination) to help the group stick together and solve its problems.

Usually, at some point a group will come to an end. The group may have accomplished its work, some group members may have moved away, or maybe it's time to join a different group. When a group has enjoyed working together, people may feel sad that the group is ending. Sometimes it helps to have a party. It might be a celebration for all the things the group has done or a time to wish everyone success in the future.

When you leave your Junior Girl Scout troop to move up to Cadette Girl Scouting, one group will have ended, but another exciting group experience will await you. More on that on pages 163–170.

Group Games

Group games help people get to know one another and help the group grow together. Here are a few ideas:

■■ PARTNERS First everyone finds a partner. Then, each pair of girls talk together for five minutes to find out all they can about each other. Each

person introduces her partner by telling the group the partner's name and sharing two interesting things she has learned about her partner.

■■ WEEKEND BEST   Each person tells the group what she most enjoys doing on weekends. The group itself might then decide to do some of the activities mentioned.

■■ FAVORITES
  ▪ Each person teaches her favorite game to the group and the group plays it.
  ▪ Each person tells the group about her favorite meal, from soup to dessert. The group can then get some of the recipes and take turns making them.
  ▪ Each person tells her favorite story to the group.

■■ DON'T TOUCH   This is a game for a group of at least ten people. Use five frisbees, or make five large, heavy cardboard circles that measure about 12 inches (30 cm.) each in diameter. One person is selected as the referee. The referee spreads out the frisbees on the ground. When she yells "go," everyone has to run to a frisbee, touch some part of it, and immediately "freeze" there. If any two people are touching each other, they are both out. The referee takes one of the frisbees out of play and calls "go" again. Everyone runs to another frisbee and touches a part of it and freezes again.

Keep playing until there's only one frisbee left and no people touching. The referee then picks one of the remaining players to be the referee for the next game.

Leadership and Troop Government

Girl Scouting gives you many opportunities to be a leader and practice leadership skills. You can plan and carry out service projects (see pages 72–73), help girls new to Girl Scouting learn its special ways, or organize some of the activities described in this handbook.

If you are a member of a Junior Girl Scout troop, you will learn a great deal about leadership and groups. With the help of your Girl Scout leaders, you and the other girls in the troop can set up your own troop government.

■ Discuss the different types of troop government, and decide which type would work best in your troop. Remember, good government makes it easier to make decisions and get things accomplished.

Below are descriptions of three troop government systems.

THE PATROL SYSTEM

A widely used form of troop government is the patrol system. In this system, your troop divides into small groups with five to eight girls in each. These small groups are called **patrols.**

Suppose your troop has twenty girls. You might have four patrols with five girls in each, or three patrols with six or seven girls in each. Here are some ways to decide which girls will be in each patrol:

- By numbers. Suppose your troop decides to have four patrols with five girls in each one. Write the number 1 on five slips of paper, the number 2 on five slips of paper, and so on. Have each girl pick a slip out of a bag. The number each girl picks is the patrol to which she will belong.
- By interests. Each girl lists her interests. Pick out the ones that are shared by the largest numbers of girls. Form patrols around each of these interests, with each girl volunteering to join the patrol that appeals to her most.

Making new friends is part of the fun of Girl Scouting. It may be a good idea to organize into new patrols from time to time.

How a Patrol Works

Each patrol can choose its own name and can make up an emblem to be used on the patrol's flag or its equipment.

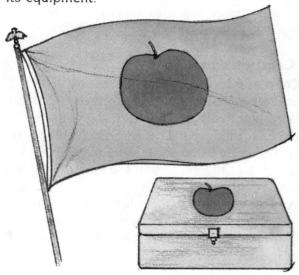

For each patrol, choose a patrol leader and an assistant patrol leader. Decide how patrol leaders and assistant leaders should be chosen in the future and how long they should serve. Switching leaders from time to time gives more girls a chance to hold office.

The patrol leader organizes the patrol, helps new members, keeps a record of dues and attendance for the girls in the patrol, leads discussions, and represents her patrol at Court of Honor meetings. (The Court of Honor is described on page 70.)

The patrol leader receives the **patrol leader cord** at an installation ceremony held by the entire troop. The cord is made up of two gold circles. The

larger one stands for the whole troop; the smaller one stands for the patrol. The cord is worn on the left shoulder.

The assistant patrol leader helps the patrol leader at meetings and does the patrol leader's job when she is absent.

The Court of Honor

The **Court of Honor** is a committee made up of the Girl Scout troop leader, the patrol leaders, the troop secretary, and the troop treasurer. The patrol leaders serve on this committee as representatives of their patrols. The troop secretary is responsible for taking notes at meetings, and the troop treasurer keeps records of the troop's money.

At Court of Honor meetings, held before or after regular meetings, decisions are made for the whole troop. The responsibilities of the Court of Honor include:

- Suggesting plans that patrols will discuss and vote on
- Asking for ideas and suggestions from patrols
- Setting up a troop kaper chart (job chart) with assignments for each patrol (see page 72 for more information).

Sometimes, Court of Honor meetings are open to all troop members. By attending these meetings, members can find out how the Court of Honor works and watch the leaders of their troop in action.

THE EXECUTIVE BOARD SYSTEM

Another type of troop government is the executive board system. In this system, the whole troop votes for a group of girls to represent them. The elected group is called an **executive board.** (The group may also be called a steering committee.) The board makes plans based on the feelings and ideas of the entire troop.

An executive board can have a president, a vice president, a secretary, a treasurer, and any other officers who are needed. The number and type of officers depend on how many girls are in the troop, how many activities and projects the troop plans to do, and what the troop feels the responsibilities of the executive board should be.

The members of the executive board usually meet alone. Sometimes, however, the board might have an open meeting in front of the other troop members.

THE TOWN MEETING SYSTEM

In the **town meeting system** of troop government, everyone participates in decision-making and leadership. Ideas, opinions, and suggestions may be offered by anyone.

With this system, you need a moderator to guide group discussions. You and the other troop members will decide how to choose a discussion moderator. Will a moderator be elected by the whole troop for a specific period of time? Will she be a girl whose name is drawn at random? Will a different girl serve as moderator for each discussion? Your troop might also want to choose girls to serve as troop treasurer and secretary.

Making Plans in Girl Scouting

Below are four steps your troop can use in planning its activities.

STEP 1: SHARE IDEAS AND COME UP WITH NEW ONES

Each girl has ideas about what she would like to do in Girl Scouting. Here are some ways for the members of a troop or group to share their ideas:

■ Make a Dream Box for ideas. Whenever someone says "I wish we could . . . ," jot down her idea and put it in the box. Next time the troop is looking for ideas, you'll have a boxful.

■ Have a brainstorming session. First, have everyone say what she would like to do, no matter how silly or impossible it may sound. Nobody should judge the ideas when they are given. One girl is chosen as the recorder—she writes down all the ideas as people mention them. Later, the troop can make decisions about whether and how to carry out the ideas.

■ Have a planning meeting. Each girl describes or shows a picture, drawing, or sample of an activity she would like the group to do.

STEP 2: MAKE DECISIONS

After a brainstorming session, the group may find that there are more good ideas than it can use.

Here are some things to remember when the group is trying to decide which ideas to carry out:

- Everyone should have a chance to speak.
- Only one person should talk at a time.
- Everyone should listen to the person who is talking, rather than interrupting.
- Everyone should try to make her points quickly and not talk too long or too much.
- Everyone's comments should be considered.
- Only one topic at a time should be discussed.

Group decisions can be made in different ways. For example, try these steps:

1. Look over the list of ideas that the group has come up with. Try to cut down your list to the things the group really wants to do. To do this, combine similar activities, and eliminate activities that don't seem likely to work for the group.

2. Collect information about any activity that the group members don't know much about.

3. Discuss the good and bad points of each activity.

4. Figure out which activities cost money to carry out and how much is needed.

5. After careful consideration of all the ideas suggested, you are ready to make final decisions about what to do. Such decisions can be made by voting. Group members could raise their hands, stand up, or write their choices on pieces of paper.

STEP 3: PLAN YOUR CALENDAR

Once activities have been chosen, you will need to make a calendar showing when they will be carried out.

Below is a sample list of activities that a group might do. The list also shows how much time each activity will take. Some activities may take up only part of a meeting, while others may last through several meetings.

When your group is ready, prepare a list like the one below. Then make a calendar for whatever time period your group decides on for the activities. Start with dates you have chosen for special events, like a Juliette Low birthday celebration.

STEP 4: PUT YOUR PLANS INTO ACTION

In order to put your plans into action, it is important to know exactly what jobs must be done and

Activity	Time Needed
Visit a local hospital to learn about medical careers.	1 meeting
Put on a puppet show for a Juliette Gordon Low birthday celebration.	6 meetings (for rehearsing, making puppets and scenery, preparing invitations, etc.)
Have a family sports day.	3 meetings
Make rice paper.	Half of a meeting
Practice sketching trail maps.	1 meeting
Plan a weekend camping trip.	2 meetings
Learn folk dances and songs, and teach them at a senior citizens' center.	3 meetings

who will do them. Activities are more fun and worthwhile when every girl knows what is expected of her and does her part. There may be jobs (such as cleaning up after a party) that are not really enjoyable, but need to get done. These jobs can be rotated so that the same people don't have them each time. The jobs can be divided by individuals, by pairs, by patrols, or by committees.

In Girl Scouting, a job is called a **kaper** and the list of jobs and who does them is called a **kaper chart.** Here are some ideas for different kinds of kaper charts.

Kaper Chart for a Troop Meeting

🍎	☀️	☘️	⭐
Aug. 6	Check all supplies	Lecture plans	Sing-along	Troop meeting
Aug. 13	Slide show plans	Check supplies	Book lecture hall	Check supplies
Aug. 20	morning meeting	Clean lecture hall	Chairs for show	Slide show

Kaper Chart for a Camping Trip

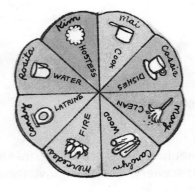

■ ■ Make a kaper chart for one of the activities that your own troop plans to do.

EVALUATING WHAT WAS DONE

After an activity is over, the members of your troop can discuss their feelings about it. Was it fun? Do all of you feel that you learned something interesting? Would you like to do this, or something like it, again? What changes would you make if you did it another time?

Troop Dues

Girl Scout troops need money for all kinds of things—project supplies, trips, games, books, and equipment. Most troops have found that a good way to pay for these things is through troop dues. A troop treasurer can be chosen to collect dues from members at each meeting. The troop might decide to deposit its money in a bank. If this is done, money can be withdrawn from the account when needed.

Before deciding how much the dues should be, the troop will need to discuss:

- How much money will be needed for the kinds of activities that are planned.
- What supplies or equipment the troop will need and how much these items will cost.
- How much the troop members feel they can afford.
- Other sources of troop money (like Girl Scout cookie sales).

Set dues at an amount that everyone in the troop feels is fair. The troop might decide to change the amount later on, if it turns out to be too low or too high.

Sometimes troop dues aren't enough for all of the activities planned and supplies needed. The troop can either trim its plans to fit the budget or can plan a special project to earn the additional money that's needed. Many Girl Scouts put their planning and budgeting skills into action when they participate in a Girl Scout cookie sale, or in a sale involving other types of products. Your Girl Scout leader can help the troop plan its money-earning activities.

Service in Girl Scouting

Service means doing something helpful without asking for or expecting a reward. Girl Scouts and Girl Guides all over the world have designed and carried out a wide variety of service projects.

A service project might take a lot of time (like clearing a vacant lot and helping to build a playground on it), or it might be something less complicated (like helping a younger girl with her homework). Service projects can be completed alone or with a group of people. Giving service is one way to demonstrate your leadership qualities.

PLANNING A SERVICE PROJECT

To help you decide what kinds of service projects you want to do, try answering these questions.

- What am I good at? What are my interests?
- What are the needs of my community?
- Who could help me?
- How much time can I devote to a service project?

Think about your answers to these questions and try to come up with an idea for a service project. In developing your plan, you'll have to ask one more important question: Will you need money to complete the project? If your answer is yes, how will you get it?

CARRYING OUT A SERVICE PROJECT

Once all the plans have been made, it's time to carry out the service project. Don't be discouraged if changes have to be made in your plan. This often is necessary once a plan is put into action. Perhaps someone who you thought would lend a hand can't do it and now you need to look for help from other people.

After completing the service project, think about which parts of the project worked and which parts didn't. This information will help you when planning future service projects.

SOME IDEAS FOR SERVICE PROJECTS

■ Below are some ideas for service projects. You might be able to do some on your own, but others would need the cooperation of several people.

- Start a story hour at the local library.
- Help someone learn to read.
- Run errands for a person in your community who is elderly and cannot get out on her own.
- Teach someone to use a computer.
- Help someone learn to speak a new language.
- Organize a physical fitness program.
- Organize a stop smoking campaign.

Growing in Groups

As the members of your group get greater experience in working together, you will find Girl Scouting more and more rewarding. You will have increasing opportunities to develop your own leadership abilities, while continuing to enjoy being part of a group.

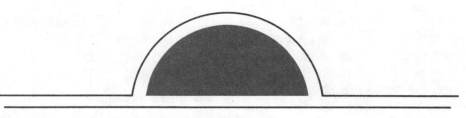

CHAPTER 6

People

Have you ever wondered how many languages are spoken in the world? How many different types of animals and plants exist? How many different places there are to live?

We live in a diverse world. Even in your local community you can find a great deal of diversity. Some people have curly hair, others have straight hair; some have red hair, others have brown hair. Many people speak English; some may speak another language. What other types of diversity can you find in your community?

People in the United States: Our Heritage of Diversity

There are many ways in which our country is diverse. Look at a map of the United States and you'll see great diversity in geography. The country reaches from the frozen north into tropical ocean waters. It has mountains, valleys, lakes, deserts, islands, and two oceans on its borders.

The United States is like a mosaic—settlers from around the world have added pieces to make up the whole picture. Across the country you will find differences in art, music, literature, styles of dress, customs, how words are pronounced, even what language is spoken. As people move about and share their cultures (ways of living), new pieces are added to the mosaic.

The earliest people who populated the United States were the American Indians (or Native Americans). Their cultures were built around what the land had to offer in terms of food and shelter.

■ Find out about the American Indians who first settled or are now living in your area. Learn about their special customs and spiritual values.

■ Write about your personal heritage. Where has your family come from?

75

■ Start a new family tradition. A tradition is a practice that is handed down from one generation to the next. For instance, a family might always have turkey with corn bread stuffing for Thanksgiving, or might always celebrate the Fourth of July with a chicken barbecue. Think of a tradition you would like to start for your family and put it into practice. It could be anything from eating dinner by candlelight once a month to giving each other homemade cards on holidays.

A MULTICULTURAL COUNTRY

The United States is multicultural—that is, made up of people with many different cultures. The cultures of the American Indians and of people from continents like Europe, Asia, and Africa have contributed in many ways to the quality of life in the United States today.

■ Take a community survey. Interview your friends and neighbors to find out about their cultural heritage. Make a collage of pictures to show the diversity of cultures in your community.

People Around the World

Although people might look different and have different customs and traditions, everyone has the same basic needs—like food, clothes, a place to live, and others to love and care about them.

■■ Visit another country through books. Read about what the people are like. Find out something about their culture. Try to figure out how climate and the resources of the land affect the lives of these people.

OTHER LANGUAGES

People with different cultures often differ in the languages they speak. One reason to learn other languages in school is to be able to communicate with many more people.

■■ Learn to speak a few words in another language. If possible, pick a language that is spoken by some people in your own community. Or choose a language that is used in a place you would like to visit. Ask someone to teach you the words in that language which mean:

Hello	My name is . . .
Goodbye	I like you
Yes	Do you need help?
No	Thank you

Sign Languages

Formal sign language was first developed in France about 200 years ago for people who were deaf or had trouble hearing. In a sign language, hand signals or gestures are used to stand for words or ideas. Like all other languages, sign languages have sets of rules.

Sign languages may differ from country to country. The type used in the United States is called American Sign Language. Since some words in English are not part of American Sign Language, people with hearing problems may also use an alphabet of finger gestures to spell out those words.

■■ Learn the finger spelling alphabet shown below and practice using it.

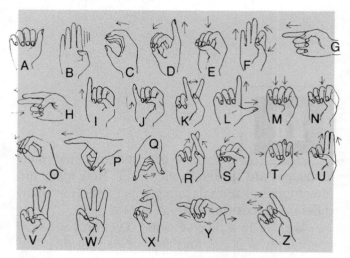

■■ Learn to make some of the signs pictured below so you can begin to speak to a deaf person.

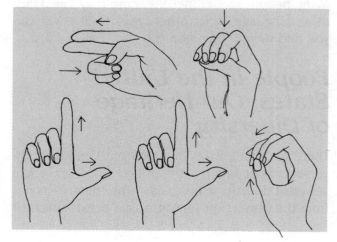

Celebrating with Our Global Neighbors

During the late fall and winter months, many cultures have special celebrations that are part of their customs and traditions. Here are some of the best-known celebrations.

The Chinese New Year

The Chinese New Year is celebrated by Chinese people all over the world as a joyous festival. Children receive gifts of money in red envelopes. Many of the decorations are also red since that color is the symbol of happiness. The celebration lasts for fifteen days and ends with the Lantern Festival. During that festival, a parade of paper lanterns led by a paper dragon winds its way through the streets.

■■ Make red decorations or wrap gifts in red to celebrate the Chinese New Year.

Three Kings Day

On the evening of January 5th, many Spanish-speaking people begin their celebration of Three Kings Day. The name refers to the kings who, in the Christian tradition, traveled by camel to bring gifts when Christ was born. Children gather fresh grass (to symbolize food for the camels) and place it in their homes, often in shoeboxes under their beds. In the morning, gifts have been left in place of the grass and the celebration continues all day with delicious food and music.

Kwanza

Kwanza, which means "first fruits," is a week-long holiday celebrated by many Black American families. It begins on December 26th and includes parties, the sharing of gifts, and a ceremony in which people take turns drinking from a single cup. Each day, a candle-lighting ceremony is held to represent a special value. One value that is celebrated is "Umoja," which means unity or togetherness.

■■ With your family or Girl Scout troop, plan and hold a candle-lighting ceremony to celebrate a value that is important to you.

Hanukkah

Hanukkah, the Festival of Lights, is a joyous holiday that lasts for eight days in late November or

December. The holiday celebrates a great victory of religious freedom won at the Jewish Temple of Jerusalem over 2,000 years ago. Today, Jewish families light candles each night of Hanukkah as a symbol of light and joy. Many children receive a four-sided top called a dreidel and other gifts during this holiday.

■ ■ Make a dreidel or some other small toy as a gift to give to a child during the holiday season.

What celebrations do you and your family participate in during the winter season?

Multicultural Festivals

■ ■ A multicultural festival can be a wonderful way to learn about and celebrate different cultures. It can be a small simple event honoring just one or two countries, or a large event requiring several months of planning. It can be given as a party with international games and activities. It can also be a good way to introduce new friends to Girl Scouting.

Planning and decision-making are key ingredients for making your festival a success. Take advantage of everyone's talent. You might need:

musicians	directors
dancers	writers
poets	actors
decorators	crafts people
makeup artists	cooks
publicists	researchers

Those taking part in the festival can be divided into groups of two or more to plan and prepare activities for each country's contributions. People who have specific talents, such as musicians or writers, could help more than one group. Use your library for resource materials. Get to know each country well, including its foods, crafts, special traditions, and styles of dress. Be sure to talk to friends and families for additional information.

In planning your festival, you will need to make decisions about:

- How long the festival will last and how the time will be spent. You might plan time for group dances, parades, fashion shows, plays, storytelling.
- Whom to invite. You might ask school friends, people from the community and from ethnic organizations, neighbors, relatives, other Girl Scouts.
- The location. Your setup might include food tables, craft booths, entertainment and dancing areas, a game area, a display area, wall space (to be decorated), booths or tables for each country or ethnic group.

Consider setting up a public relations committee. The people in this group could work on ways to let others know about your event. Announcements, posters, fliers, newsletters, and personal letters are all possibilities.

SOME IDEAS FOR YOUR FESTIVAL

Japan

■ Serve tea Japanese-style on large floor cushions. Read about the tea ceremony *chanoyu* and serve the finely powdered green tea that is used.

■ Compose haiku poetry. A haiku is a short, three-line poem that does not rhyme. It contains seventeen syllables and usually describes a feeling, something in nature, or a season of the year. Here are the requirements for a haiku:

- First line: 5 syllables.
- Second line: 7 syllables.
- Third line: 5 syllables.

Often, the first line describes the setting, the second line describes the action, and the third line expresses the feeling or gives the ending of the situation.

Examples:

An April morning
The sun is shining
  brightly.
My heart wildly
  beats.

The rushing water
Tosses a shimmering
  fish.
A silver flash gone.

Nigeria

■ ■ Tie-dye your own T-shirt. Tie-dyeing is an old art that was first perfected by the Nigerians. They used natural colors from roots and plants to dye material. Use rubber bands to tie sections of the T-shirt to form peaks. The places that have the rubber bands will resist the dye. Dip the cloth into the dye; the longer it soaks, the darker the color will be. Remove the rubber bands and rinse in cold water. You can use more than one color. Begin with the lightest color and go through each step for every color.

India

A mosaic is a picture made from small pieces of material (tile, clay, stones).

■ ■ Make your own colorful mosaics. First draw your design on some cardboard or plywood. Then glue on small pieces of material (birdseed, tiny pebbles, sand, tree bark chips, fruit seeds, or any other small pieces of material). Varnish the finished mosaic.

United States

Many fine quilts have been made in the United States. Some designs for quilts involve the land and surroundings—for example, log cabins, barns, windmills, the sun, corn, and flowers. Folk art museums have some of these quilts on display. One popular type of quilt is the "crazy quilt," which makes use of scraps of fabric with different textures and colors. The pieces are sewn together to make a beautiful new blanket.

■ ■ Make a quilt with some friends to display at your multicultural festival.

You will need: 48 8-inch (20 cm.) fabric squares, a flat sheet or piece of fabric 64 inches × 48 inches (160 cm. × 120 cm.) for the backing, embroidery yarn, thread, needles, batting (or some other filling). Follow these steps:

1. Stitch 8 of the squares together to form a row. Repeat, until you have used all the squares and have formed six rows. Sew all the rows together to form the top of the quilt.

2. Cut the sheet so that it is the same size as the top of the quilt. This piece will be the bottom of the quilt.

3. Using a blanket stitch or back stitch (see page 90), sew the top and bottom pieces together. Insert the batting in the quilt before you have completely sewn the top and bottom pieces together.

4. Tie knots in each corner of each square and in the center of each square. The diagram shows you how the knots should look.

INTERNATIONAL RECIPES

■■ Try serving some of these dishes at your multicultural festival.

American Indian Corn Pudding

Ingredients

4 eggs	2 teaspoons salt
½ cup butter	1 teaspoon pepper
⅔ cup flour	4 cups corn (fresh or canned)
2 cups milk	butter to grease a baking dish

Directions

1. Preheat oven to 350°.

2. Separate eggs. Beat whites until stiff, not dry.

3. Melt butter in a medium-sized pan. Stir flour in quickly over medium heat until a smooth paste forms.

4. Stir the paste constantly while adding milk, and allow the mixture to boil.

5. Lower the heat. Add yolks, salt, pepper, and corn. Mix.

6. Turn off the heat. Fold in egg whites with a rubber spatula.

7. Grease a baking dish with butter and pour in the mixture.

8. Bake 35 minutes or until it is lightly browned.

(Serves 12)

Chinese Velvet Corn Soup

Ingredients

2 eggs
2 tablespoons milk
3 cups chicken broth (canned or made from bouillon cubes)
1 small can of creamed corn (8½ or 8¾ oz.)
1 tablespoon cornstarch

Directions

1. Separate the whites and yolks of the eggs. You will only need the egg whites.

2. Beat the egg whites and milk together and put aside.

3. Boil the chicken broth over high heat.

4. Add the corn to the broth. Stir until it comes to a second boil.

5. Dissolve the cornstarch in two tablespoons of cold water. Pour the mixture into the soup.

6. While the soup is cooking, stir it until it thickens.

7. Take the soup off the heat and pour in the egg white mixture. Stir a few times and serve. (Serves 4)

Hungarian Körözöt Dip

Ingredients

8 ounces cream cheese
12 ounces sour cream
1½ tablespoons freeze-dried chives
1 tablespoon paprika
½ teaspoon salt
½ small yellow onion finely chopped

Directions

   1. Allow the cream cheese to stand at room temperature until it softens. Put it in a bowl.

   2. Add the sour cream and mix with the cream cheese until smooth.

   3. Add the rest of the ingredients and mix well. Sprinkle a little paprika and chives on top for decoration. Keep refrigerated until ready to serve. Serve with crackers or potato chips.

Other Recipes

You can find many other international recipes such as lasagna, quiche lorraine, or latkes (potato pancakes) in cookbooks.

A MINI-WORLD CONFERENCE

■ For a better understanding of living conditions in other countries, organize a Mini-World Conference. Delegates from other countries would meet to discuss current issues—problems related to health, education, family, and school life. Some of the delegates could be girls who have recently moved here from other countries or who are visiting the United States, perhaps as part of a student exchange program. Other delegates might be Girl Scouts who have learned enough about a country to represent it. Invite neighbors and friends to attend.

INTERNATIONAL PEN PALS

■ Girl Scouts who are 10 to 17 years old can request a pen pal from Girl Scouts of the U.S.A. by getting a special form from their Girl Scout councils. You *must* use this form; otherwise, your request will not be considered. Fill out the form very neatly, in ink, and send it to Girl Scout national headquarters. (The address is on the form.) Staff members at national headquarters will then try to link you with a pen pal in one of the areas of the world that you request. However, you will have to be patient. Whether or not you will get a pen pal depends on how many other U.S.A. Girl Scouts are asking for pen pals from the same areas, and how many girls from those areas want pen pals here. Sometimes it just isn't possible to find pen pals for everyone. If you are one of the lucky girls who does get a pen pal, it will still take at least six months; but the wait will be worth it, because many Girl Scout/Girl Guide pen pals correspond for years and become life-long friends.

Other Types of Diversity

Besides differing in the languages they speak, foods they eat, and holidays they celebrate, people differ in the skills and abilities they have and in the experiences they've gone through. Being able to enjoy, learn from, and work with many different kinds of people is a valuable ability.

ELDERLY PEOPLE

■ Elderly people have learned so much in their lifetimes that they have a great deal to share with younger people. In addition to the talents and abilities they have, many of them are still learning new skills and hobbies, or are beginning new careers. Here are some ideas for activities:

- Invite senior citizens to be speakers, chaperones, and guests at Girl Scout activities.
- Study how older people are portrayed on television programs, in movies, and in books. Are they represented as a diverse group of individuals, or do they all seem to be the same type?

- Ask a retired person to help you with a service project you would like to do in your community.
- Find out more about the special problems and special joys of growing old by talking to neighbors and relatives.
- Ask a senior citizen to share her knowledge of a subject or activity that interests you, such as a foreign language, gardening, art, travel, or community history.

PEOPLE WITH DISABILITIES

A person with a disability is "unable" to do certain things. She may have trouble hearing, seeing, talking, learning, or walking. Or the person may have a special health problem like epilepsy or a heart condition.

People with disabilities are just as diverse as people without disabilities. Everyone has many abilities. Although a person with disabilities finds it hard to do some things, otherwise she is like

anybody else—her other abilities are not affected. If she is blind, she may "read" by using braille, a special type of printing in which raised dots are felt by the fingers. She can still talk, play games, solve math problems, and do all the other things that do

not require vision. If a person has trouble walking, she might need special equipment to get around. She can still make crafts, perform a science experiment, operate a computer, prepare a meal, and have fun with her friends. The abilities of people always outnumber their physical disabilities.

In 1917, some girls in a New York City home for children with disabilities decided that they wanted to be Girl Scouts. Their leader made arrangements for them to meet with a group of girls who did not have disabilities. Since then, many Girl Scouts with and without disabilities have worked together on badges and projects.

Find out more about disabilities:

■■ Read about people with disabilities like writer Helen Keller, President Franklin Delano Roosevelt, composer Ludwig van Beethoven, and Juliette Gordon Low, the founder of Girl Scouting.

■ ■ ■ Learn about the special equipment some people use—for example, hearing aids, wheelchairs, special utensils for eating, braille books.

■ ■ Create dramatic skits about disabilities. Girls with and without disabilities can work together to write and perform their plays. The section on play production (pages 143–144) may help you in planning this project.

■ ■ Survey your community or your school to find out how easy or hard it is for people with disabilities to get around. If you can think of ways to get rid of an obstacle, share your ideas with a community or school official.

The World of People

As you have learned, the world is rich with a variety of people with different customs, languages, talents, and abilities. People live in other places with different hopes, dreams, and desires. But in spite of these differences, we have much in common. We all laugh, work, play, and share the resources of this world.

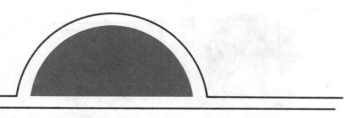

CHAPTER 7

Day by Day— Skills for Living

Each day is the start of a whole new set of experiences. The more skills for living you have, the better able you will be to meet the opportunities and challenges that arise. On any given day, you may need to decide how to look your best, how to spend your time and money, what to do if an emergency occurs, what and when to eat, how to repair things, and how to act in the out-of-doors. In this chapter you will learn ways to care for yourself in a confident, responsible way.

Looking Your Best

PERSONAL CARE

Looking your best by taking care of yourself—your hair, teeth, skin, hands, nails, and feet—is a way of showing that you feel good about yourself. Personal care can be easy when you set up a routine and follow it every day so that it becomes a habit.

Hair

Shampoo your hair and massage your scalp as often as needed—perhaps every day, perhaps twice a week or so.

■ There are different types of hair—oily, normal, and dry. Find out what type your hair is, how often you should wash it, and what kinds of shampoos and conditioners are best for you.

■ Try styling your hair in different ways to see which is most flattering for you. Look through magazines to find some styles you might want to try. Ask others for their opinions about how the different hairstyles look on you.

plaque, which is a combination of saliva, bacteria, and food particles that can cause cavities if allowed to remain on the teeth. To remove plaque, brush your teeth after meals (or if that isn't possible, rinse your mouth) and floss your teeth at least once a day.

■ Make your own hair decorations by twisting two or three ribbons around a plain barrette or hair clip. Use a small amount of glue to hold the ends of the ribbons in place. Or, braid the ribbons and your hair together.

Here are more tips to help keep your teeth clean and healthy:

- Eat snacks like apples, celery, carrots.
- Avoid sweet snacks like sticky candy, soda pop, gum.
- Visit the dentist for regular checkups and cleanings. Ask your dentist to show you the proper way to brush and floss your teeth.

Skin

■ Skin, the outer covering of your body, provides protection in a number of ways. For one thing, your skin keeps you cool when it is hot and helps warm you when it is cold.

Here are some tips on skin care:

- Your face and hands have more exposure to dirt and germs than other parts of the body, and so they need to be washed several times or more each day.
- Using a lotion or skin cream after bathing can help to keep your skin moist and smooth.
- For some girls, an astringent lotion applied to oily areas of the skin can help prevent skin problems.
- Use a deodorant, if you need it, to help control your underarm perspiration.

Teeth

With proper care of your teeth, you can help them stay clean and healthy. It is important to remove

■ Make your own perfumed body powder. Mix 5 to 10 drops of your favorite bath oil or cologne (one drop at a time) with one cup of talcum or unscented baby powder. Use it after a bath or shower to feel extra special!

SOME FACTS ABOUT CIGARETTES, ALCOHOL, AND DRUGS

Most people know that smoking cigarettes is very dangerous because it can lead to lung cancer, heart disease, and other health problems. Smoking can also have negative effects on a person's appearance. It causes skin to wrinkle sooner and leaves yellow stains on the hands and teeth. In addition, people who smoke usually smell like cigarettes—the odor gets in their hair and clothing and on their breath. Nicotine, the drug found in cigarette tobacco, is addictive. Many people who start smoking have a very hard time quitting.

Drinking alcohol—beer, wine, or liquor—is also very harmful to young people. Often times, it causes damage to the liver, heart, and brain. Drinking has many other negative effects as well. Alcohol slows down the reactions of the brain and the body, which is why it is dangerous for people to drive after drinking. Some people who drink alcohol find it impossible to stop; they become alcoholics and may cause great harm to themselves and others. Trained help is needed to help them quit drinking.

Alcohol is just one of the drugs that can damage your body. Many other drugs can cause harm, such as marijuana, heroin, and cocaine. Sometimes, people are encouraged by their peers to try cigarettes, alcohol, or other harmful drugs. By being aware of the health facts, you'll be best able to deal with this type of situation if it occurs. Ask your parents, a teacher, or your Girl Scout leader for more information.

For activities related to appearance, try the Looking Your Best and Healthy Living badges in this book (pages 174 and 178) and the Personal Health and Art to Wear badges in *Girl Scout Badges and Signs*.

CLOTHING

Everyone has her own fashion sense. The styles and colors of clothing you choose to wear can be an expression of your special interests, tastes, and feelings about yourself.

Keeping clothes clean and neat is another way of expressing how you feel about yourself. Below are some tips on washing, drying, and repairing clothes.

Washing and Drying Your Clothes

■■ Here are some things to remember about washing and drying clothes, whether you are doing them by hand or in a machine.

- Check the care label inside the item of clothing. It will tell you the water temperature to use for washing and how to dry the clothing.
- Empty the contents of all pockets before doing a wash.

- Rub a small amount of laundry detergent or a prewashing liquid on any stains, and soak the item of clothing for several minutes before washing.
- Follow the directions on the detergent box to decide how much to use.
- Some clothes (especially those with synthetic fibers) will not need ironing if you remove them immediately from the washer or dryer and then hang or fold them neatly.

Clothing Repairs

By becoming skilled at clothing repairs, you can make many things look like new. Put together a sewing kit so you will be ready.

MAKE A SEWING KIT

■■ The main things you will want to store in the kit are:

- a package of assorted needles—the heavier the fabric, the thicker the needle you will need
- a thimble
- a small box of straight pins
- scissors
- spools of thread—different colors and thicknesses
- a pin cushion
- a small ruler or measuring tape
- iron-on patches

To store the supplies, you could use a metal container (like a cookie tin) or a shoebox that is decorated with attractive paper or paint.

Sewing stitches. The diagrams below illustrate the basic sewing stitches. Before starting to sew, it is helpful to fix the fabric in place with straight pins. Some people prefer to use a thimble when sewing by hand. Try using a thimble either on the finger you use to push the needle through the fabric or on the finger that the point of the needle will touch.

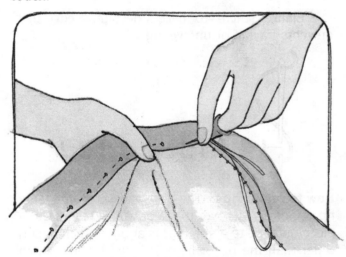

Hemming stitch—for hemming pants, dresses, and skirts

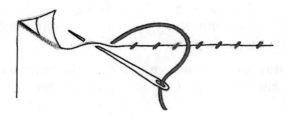

Basting stitch—for holding fabric in place before doing the final sewing

Running stitch—for straight seams

Back stitch—for extra-strong straight seams

Overcast stitch—to prevent edges from fraying or unraveling

Blanket stitch—to make a decorative edge that prevents fraying or unraveling

How to repair rips The best way to repair a large rip or hole is to cover the spot with a patch. Cut a piece of fabric to a size that is about ½ inch (1 cm) wider than the rip or hole. Use the blanket stitch (see above) around the edges of the patch to attach it to the clothing.

You can also use a ready-made iron-on patch. To attach this type of patch, follow the directions on the package.

How to make a hem Fold up the bottom of the skirt, dress, or pant legs about ¼ inch (½ cm) and

fold again to the length you want. Pin the hem in place. Before sewing, try on the garment to make sure it hangs evenly. Sew along the inside edge of the fold, on the wrong side of the clothing, using the hemming stitch (see page 89).

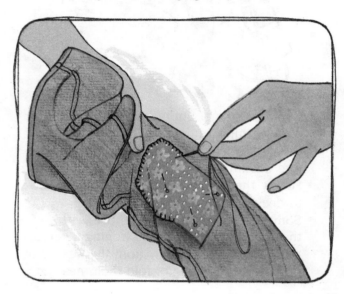

How to repair a torn seam. Seams are the edges where two pieces of fabric are joined together. To repair an open seam, turn the clothing inside out. Pin the part of the seam that needs repair. Sew along the crease made by the original thread using the running stitch or back stitch. If the fabric has started to fray or if there is less than ½ inch (1 cm) for a seam, you might want to use the blanket stitch.

How to replace a button. Mark the place for the button with two straight pins. Start from the reverse side of the fabric, so the knot in the thread is underneath. Pass the threaded needle up through the fabric and through one of the buttonholes, then through another hole and into the fabric. Repeat this six to eight times. Tie off the thread on the wrong side.

When sewing a four-hole button, weave the thread in and out of the fabric and button holes to form an "X"—this will hold the button tightly.

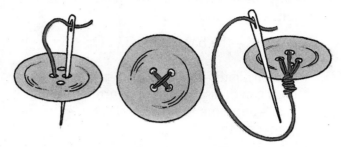

A button for a coat, jacket, or waistband should be sewed loosely. To do this, place a pin across the top of the button before you begin sewing. Sew as described above, working around the pin. When the button has been sewn on securely, remove the pin and pull the button away from the clothing. Wind the extra thread in the needle around the threads between the button and the clothing several times to make a shank. Push the needle through the fabric to bring it out on the wrong side, and tie a knot.

Nutrition

Are you what you eat? Not exactly, but the foods you eat will certainly affect you. The best diet for your health and well-being is a balanced one.

THE BASIC FOOD GROUPS

Eating foods from four basic food groups will give you a balanced diet.

FRUIT-VEGETABLE GROUP

MEAT GROUP

BREAD-CEREAL GROUP

MILK GROUP

Fruits and Vegetables

Fruits and vegetables are the plants you eat. Fruits are the plant parts that contain seeds, and they are often sweet. Some examples are strawberries, watermelon, apples, grapes, bananas, squash, tomatoes, and kiwi. Vegetables are those plant parts that are often cooked before eating. Vegetables can be very different parts of the plant. Some fruits are vegetables too. For example:

- Carrots and beets are roots.
- Asparagus and celery are stems.
- Broccoli and cauliflower are flower buds.
- Green beans and snow peas are seed cases with seeds (fruits).
- Spinach and lettuce are leaves.
- Corn and peas are seeds.

The juices made from fruits and vegetables belong in this group too.

■ Have a vegetable exploration. With a group of friends, find out about some types of vegetables that you haven't tried. Perhaps everyone could pick one vegetable to bring to a tasting party.

■■ Plant vegetable seeds and grow your own garden of fresh vegetables.

Bread and Cereal

This food group contains grains (hard, dried seeds) like wheat, corn, rice, oats, rye, and barley. It also includes any foods made from grain flours—for example, cereal from rice flour, tortillas from corn flour, and pasta from wheat flour.

■ Explore breakfast cereals. Study the ingredients listed on different packages to find out what grains were used to make the cereals. List the different grain ingredients in each cereal.

Meat, Poultry, Fish, and Legumes

Foods in this group are very high in protein. Legumes are peas or beans like lentils, peanuts, soybeans, and pinto beans that are very high in protein and make a good substitute for fish, poultry, or meat. That is why they are in this food group rather than in the vegetable group.

■ Make a giant sandwich with a number of different foods from this group; share it with your friends.

Milk and Milk Products

The foods in this group are often called dairy products. Cream, butter, and all kinds of cheeses are included in this food group.

■ Compare different types of milk. Find out about whole milk, low-fat milk, skim milk, buttermilk, evaporated milk, powdered milk, and goat's milk. If you do this with friends, everyone can bring in one type of milk. Compare the taste, appearance, and cost of the different milks.

A BALANCED DIET

When you eat properly, you can be sure that you are getting the nutrients that your body needs. The basic nutrients in food are:

- Proteins—the basic building blocks for your body
- Carbohydrates—starches and sugar that your body can digest quickly and turn into energy.
- Fats—nutrients that the body stores for energy for later
- Vitamins and minerals—nutrients that help make your body work and prevent certain diseases
- Water—a very important part of your body. In fact, your body is more than three-fourths water. Water is in most foods and keeps your body from dehydrating (becoming too dry).

■ Keep track of the foods you eat each day to make certain you have a balanced diet.

TESTING FOODS

■■ The following activities will let you see whether a certain nutrient is present in a food. Only small amounts of food, such as scraps left over at the end of a meal, are needed for these tests. This activity might be done during an outdoor cookout.

Starch Test

When placed on food that contains starch, iodine reacts chemically with the starch to form a bluish-black compound.

To test for starch, you will need tincture of iodine and scraps of food. Put one drop of tincture of iodine on the food and watch what happens. (Iodine should be handled carefully. It will stain if it spills and is poisonous if swallowed.)

Vitamin C Test

Vitamin C reacts chemically with starch-iodine and removes the bluish-black color.

To test for vitamin C, you will need cornstarch, water, tincture of iodine, juices, and other liquids. Add one teaspoon of cornstarch to one cup of water and stir to dissolve it. Add 10 drops of tincture of iodine to the cornstarch solution. This will give you a bluish-black liquid that can be used to test for vitamin C.

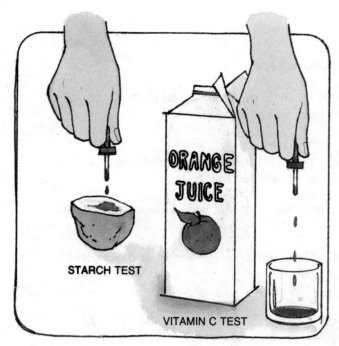

STARCH TEST

VITAMIN C TEST

To test for calcium, you will need a jar, vinegar, and a chicken bone or bits of eggshell. Vinegar removes calcium from bones and shells and softens them. Place the chicken bone or eggshells in a jar and fill it with vinegar. Change the vinegar every two or three days. After two to three weeks, check the hardness of the bone or shells.

Fat or Oil Test

Foods that have fat or oil (liquid fat) leave a greasy spot on paper because oil and fat seep into the pores and fibers, rather than evaporating as water does.

To test for fat or oil, you will need scraps of food and a piece of brown paper. (Do not use buttered or fried foods, since buttering or frying would add fats to foods that might not otherwise have contained them.) Crush a small bit of food on the brown paper. Let the paper dry. If a greasy spot remains, the food contains oil or fat.

Put 10 drops of the bluish-black test solution in a cup or small glass and add the juice or other liquid, one drop at a time. Stop after 20 drops. If vitamin C is not present, the color will stay the same. If the juice or liquid has vitamin C, the solution will lose its color. Note: Boiling destroys vitamin C. Boil a tablespoon of juice that tested as having vitamin C. Then add it to a test solution to see if the vitamin C has been destroyed.

Safety Sense

"Safety sense" means thinking carefully and acting safely. It's keeping yourself from harm, knowing how to prevent accidents, and knowing what to do when they occur.

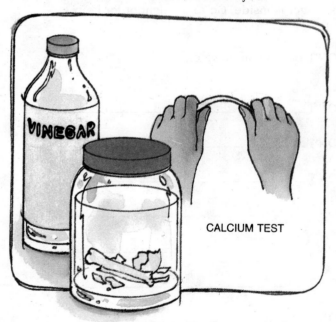

CALCIUM TEST

Calcium Test

Calcium is the mineral that adds strength and hardness to bones.

SAFETY DO'S AND DON'TS

Here is a list of safety guidelines that you should know. Discuss them with an adult and add other safety rules to this list.

If You Are Going Somewhere

DO obey traffic signals and signs, and also obey traffic police, crossing guards, and student safety patrols.

DO walk where you can see and be seen by other people.

DO follow the buddy system. When you are paired with a buddy, you can look after each other.

DO go immediately to a police officer, to an adult whom you know, or into a store if you think someone is trying to follow you.

DO wear seat belts when riding in a car, even if the trip is very short.

DO wear light or white clothing when walking at dusk or at night.

Do try to sit in a place on a bus or train where the conductor or driver can see you. Tell the driver or conductor if another passenger is bothering you or making you feel uncomfortable.

DO have your key ready—but hidden from the sight of others—so you can go right into your house or apartment.

DO carry extra change with you in case you need to make an emergency call.

DON'T walk in the roadway, on the curb, or between parked cars.

DON'T take shortcuts through dark alleys, vacant lots, or abandoned buildings.

DON'T leave your buddy or a group you are with.

DON'T take candy, gum, money, or other gifts from a stranger.

DON'T distract the driver or fool around when riding in a car or on the bus.

DON'T walk alone when it is dark.

DON'T stick your head or hands out of a car, bus, or train window or throw things out of the window.

DON'T enter your house or apartment if you think a stranger is inside. Go to a neighbor for help.

DON'T play on an elevator.

DO _____

DO _____

DO _____

DO _____

DO _____

DO _____

DO _____

DO _____

DON'T _____

DON'T _____

DON'T _____

DON'T _____

DON'T _____

DON'T _____

DON'T _____

DON'T _____

If You Are Home Alone

DO make sure you know a visitor who comes to the door, before letting him or her in.

DON'T open the door before finding out who is there. If the person is a stranger and says "I have a package" or "I need to have you sign something," don't open the door. Instead, tell the person to come back another time.

DO keep all doors and windows locked.

DO be careful what you say to a stranger on the telephone. If someone telephones for a member of your family who is not home, say something like this: "_____ can't come to the phone right now." (Don't say: "_____ isn't home right now.") Take a message, or ask the person to call back later.

DON'T let strangers know there is no one at home but you.

DO tell an adult in your home about any strange calls, visitors, or prowlers.

DON'T give a person who calls the "wrong" number your telephone number. Just say: "You have the wrong number."

DO call the police immediately if someone is prowling around your house or tries to break in.

DON'T leave your home if you think someone is prowling around or trying to break in. Make sure doors and windows are locked. Call the police.

DO _____

_____

DO _____

_____

DO _____

_____

DO _____

_____

DO _____

_____

DO _____

DON'T _____

_____

DON'T _____

_____

DON'T _____

_____

DON'T _____

_____

DON'T _____

_____

DON'T _____

If You Are in a Public or a Play Area

(The public place could be a shopping mall, movie theater, large parking lot, etc.)

DO report a person who is following you to a police officer, store salesperson, or other adult.

DON'T be afraid to scream or yell if someone tries to get you to leave with him or her.

DO pick a meeting place beforehand in case you're separated from family or friends.

DON'T wander off alone.

DO remain calm if you get lost.

DON'T go to public restrooms alone.

DON'T play in deserted or out-of-the-way places such as alleys and dead-end streets.

DON'T play around construction sites or abandoned buildings or in vacant lots.

DO _____

DON'T _____

_____

_____

Weather Safety

DO seek shelter during a storm. Stay away from tall objects like trees and poles.

DON'T stand under a tree during rain. If lightning strikes, a tree is one of the first things that may be hit.

DO dress properly. Being too hot or too cold can be harmful to you.

DON'T ignore your body's warning signals. Shivering is an early sign of hypothermia—too little body heat. Dizziness, weakness, and nausea are early warning signs of hyperthermia—too much body heat.

DO protect yourself against sunburn. Use sun blocks or sunscreens, especially if you haven't spent much time in the sun lately.

DON'T forget your skin can get sunburned before you start feeling too hot. Protect yourself in advance.

DO be ready for storms. After a storm, be careful where you walk.

DON'T touch power lines that may have fallen during a storm.

DO _____

DON'T _____

_____

_____

Personal Safety

DO remember you have rights and you can say no to things that are harmful.

DO protect private parts of your body—those covered by a bathing suit.

DO tell your parents, trusted adults, teachers, doctors, or nurses if you have been touched in a way that you feel is wrong.

DO kick, yell, or run away as fast as you can if someone tries to harm you.

DO run to a place where you can find a helpful adult: school, police station, or home.

DO _____

_____

DON'T let anyone do things to you that you don't think are right.

DON'T let someone touch you in a way that makes you feel uncomfortable.

DON'T be afraid to ask for help.

DON'T believe messages a stranger gives you like, "Your dad asked me to bring you home," or "Someone in your family is sick—come with me," or "I'll tell your parents on you if you don't do what I ask."

DON'T _____

_____

If you see something suspicious or think someone has tried to harm you, try to remember the facts:

When did it happen?
What happened?
Where did it happen?
Who was there?

Try to remember what the person(s) looked like (sex, height, weight, clothing, shoes, and color of hair, skin, and eyes). Also try to remember important details about the person's vehicle (license number, color, and model) if he or she was driving one. Be sure to report any suspicious incident to an adult.

■ SAFETY ACTIVITIES Talk about and act out what to do in these situations. Try to think of more than one solution.

- You are home alone and the phone rings. You are asked if your parents are home. What do you say?
- A man knocks on your door. He says that he has a package you must sign for. What do you do?
- Someone comes to your door and asks to use your phone to call a taxi. What do you do?
- As you are walking home from school, a man whom you don't know approaches you. He says that your mother has been in an accident and he is going to take you to the hospital to see her. What would you do?
- An adult asks you to play a game and wants you to promise to keep it a secret. What should you do?

■ Here are some other safety activities to try:

- Show that you know how to inspect and safely ride a bicycle.
- Make up a puppet show, play, or skit about the importance of wearing seat belts. Put on a performance for others.
- Create a game, song, or poem about safety.
- Make a safety checklist for a sport you like. Share your list with others.

FIRST AID

First aid is the care you give someone who is hurt or ill before medical help arrives. Knowing first aid skills and safety rules can help prevent accidents and prepare you to act in case an emergency occurs.

When an accident or emergency happens, stay calm and, if possible, get an adult to help you. If the injury is serious, call a doctor right away. Do not move an injured person unless there is danger like a fire or exposed electrical wire.

Having a first aid kit on hand and knowing how to use it can also help you be prepared.

■ With your troop or family, put together a first aid kit. Here are some items to include:

First aid book
Soap
Safety pins
Scissors
Distilled water (in an
    unbreakable
    container)
Tweezers
Sewing needle
Matches
Adhesive bandages
Flashlight
Paper drinking cups

Adhesive tape
Sterile gauze
Triangular bandage or
    clean cloth
Cotton swabs
Emergency telephone
    numbers
Change for phone calls

First Aid Guide

Use this as a guide for what to do if there is an emergency. **Always tell an adult afterwards** if you have given someone first aid.

Accident or Emergency		What to Do
Animal bite		Wash the wound with soap and warm water, and apply a clean bandage or cloth. Call a doctor or hospital.
Bleeding	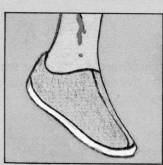	Small cuts: Clean the cut with soap and warm water, and cover with a bandage. Large wounds that will not stop bleeding: Rest a clean cloth directly on the wound and press firmly. (Use your bare hand if you have no cloth.) Apply pressure until the bleeding stops. Use adhesive tape to hold the cloth in place. Raise the bleeding part above the level of the person's heart if possible. Call a doctor.
Blisters		Wash the area with soap and warm water. Cover with a clean bandage. Do not break the blister.
Bumps and bruises	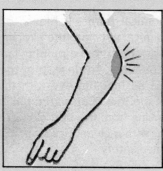	Put a cold, damp cloth on the area. If there is a lot of swelling, call an adult for help.

Accident or Emergency	What to Do

Burns

If the burn has not broken or charred the skin, rest the burned area in cold (not ice) water, pat dry, and cover with a clean cloth. (Do not use ointment, butter, or petroleum jelly.) Have an adult check the burn. Call a doctor or the hospital if the skin is broken, blistered, or charred.

Choking
Let others know by signaling with your hand across your throat

If the person can speak, cough, or breathe, do nothing. Otherwise, stand behind the person and grasp your hands around her, just under her rib cage. Press your hands into her stomach with four quick upward moves. Do this until the person spits out the stuck food or object.

Eye injuries

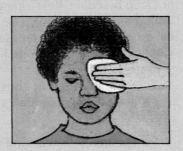

When a person gets hit in the eye, put a cold, clean cloth over it. Have the eye checked by a doctor.

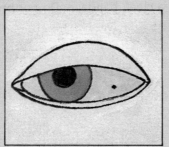

Foreign objects: If small objects (like an eyelash or piece of dirt) get into the eye, do not allow the person to rub her eye. Use a cup filled with cold water to rinse the eye. (Do this over a sink if possible.) Have the person bend so that her head is sideways. Pour water over the opened eye, and tell the person to move her eyeball up and down. If an object is sticking into the eyeball, do not attempt to remove it. Call a doctor or hospital immediately.

Chemical burns: If bleach or some other cleaning chemical gets into the eye, immediately rinse it with cool water (from a running faucet or cup) for at least 15 minutes. To rinse, turn the person's head to the side so that the eye with the chemical burn is on the bottom. Let water run slowly across the eye starting from the part closest to the nose. Cover the eye with a clean, dry cloth. Call a doctor or hospital immediately.

Accident or Emergency	What to Do

Fainting

Help the person lie down or bend over with her head between her knees. Loosen tight clothing. Wipe her face with cool water. Call a doctor if the person doesn't open her eyes quickly.

Fractures, sprains, broken bones

Do not move the injured person. Keep the person calm. Call a doctor or hospital.

Frostbite: Part of the body starts to freeze. The skin turns white or grayish yellow.

As quickly as possible, warm the area. Put the frozen area into warm (not hot) water. Dry very gently (do not rub or press hard) and wrap in warm cloth, blankets, or both. Call a doctor.

Hyperthermia (too much body heat): Heat exhaustion is mild, heat stroke is severe.

Cool off, get out of the sun. Slowly drink cool (not cold) water. Call a doctor if the person is very hot, not sweating, pale, nauseous, has trouble breathing, and seems dazed and not sure of what is happening.

Hypothermia (too little body heat)

Come inside and warm up as quickly as possible. Move around quickly. Sip a hot beverage or eat hot foods.

Insect bites, stings

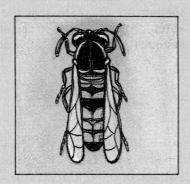

Remove the stinger if you can. Don't use tweezers, as this may cause poison to be pumped into the bitten area. Instead, scrape sideways with your finger. Wash the area with soap and water, and apply ice to reduce the swelling. Put calamine lotion on to stop the pain and itching. If there is a lot of swelling, or if the person seems to be getting sick or showing signs of shock, there may be an allergic reaction. In this case, call a doctor or hospital immediately.

Nosebleed

Have the person sit forward on a chair with her head bent slightly forward. Pinch the lower part of her nose for at least five minutes to stop the bleeding. Then place a cold, wet cloth on her nose and face.

Poisoning

Call your local poison control center or a doctor for help immediately.

Shock (can occur in any kind of emergency): You may notice sweating, rapid breathing, nausea, and cold or clammy skin.

Keep the person lying down. Elevate the feet. Place one cloth or blanket under the person and another cloth or blanket over her. Try to keep her comfortable and calm. Call a doctor.

Splinter

Gently wash the area with clean water. Look for the edge of the splinter and try to pull it out using your fingertips or tweezers. Be careful not to push the splinter under the skin.

Sunburn

Prevent sunburn by using sunscreens. Look for lotions or creams with an SPF number of 8 or higher. Limit your time in the sun and remember that sunburns can happen on hazy, cloudy days too. If a sunburn occurs, gently soak the burned area in cold water. (Do not put ice on the area.) If the person is in a great deal of pain, call a doctor.

FIRST AID ACTIVITIES

■ Complete the First Aid badge in *Girl Scout Badges and Signs*.

■ Complete a first aid course that is offered in your community.

PREPARING FOR POSSIBLE EMERGENCIES

An emergency is a situation that needs very fast action. It may be a dangerous situation like a fire or a gas leak, or a serious accident like poisoning or a broken bone. It could be a life-threatening illness, such as a heart attack or a very severe asthma attack or allergic reaction.

Knowing whom to call in an emergency is very important. Having a list of emergency numbers ready in advance can be a life-saver.

■ Make a list like the one on page 103, and post copies next to each telephone in your home. Look up the numbers in the phone book or ask an adult for help. Keep your list up-to-date, and add other telephone numbers as you think of them.

Emergency Phone Numbers

Mom (or guardian) at work   _____

Dad (or guardian) at work   _____

Other relatives:

    (Name) _____   _____

    (Name) _____   _____

Neighbors:

    (Name) _____   _____

    (Name) _____   _____

Police   _____

Doctor   _____

Dentist   _____

Fire department   _____

Ambulance or rescue squad   _____

Poison control center   _____

Electric company   _____

Gas company   _____

Oil company   _____

Taxi   _____

Other important numbers:

_____   _____

_____   _____

_____   _____

_____   _____

■ Practice making emergency phone calls with an adult. (Do not use a real telephone.) Learn how to give the most important information quickly and how to follow directions given to you. Here are a few situations to think about:

- Your classmate has fallen down the stairs and needs medical help.
- Your friend's little brother drank some ammonia.
- Your neighbor's house is on fire.
- Someone is trying to break into your home.
- The lights in the house have gone out.

■ Find out if and where the following are in your home:

- the fuse box or circuit breaker box
- the main water valve
- the furnace or hot water heater
- the thermostat

Find out emergency procedures for one of the above. For example; learn how to shut off the water.

■ Look through your home for things that might be poisonous, such as medicines, cleaning fluids, plants, and cosmetics. With the help of an adult, label all poisons and store them in a safe place—out of the reach of young children.

FIRE SAFETY

Fires can and do happen each day. You can help protect yourself and your family by learning about ways to prevent fires and to plan for possible emergencies.

Preventing Fires

■ Check for and correct some of these common fire hazards:

- Electrical outlets with too many plugs
- Portable heaters near curtains or fabric chairs and sofas
- Paint and cleaning supplies stored in hot, crowded spaces
- Newspapers stacked in large piles
- Frayed electrical cords
- Appliances used with extension cords for long periods of time
- Dirty, oily, or paint-stained rags piled together
- Curtains or towels hanging very close to an oven or stove top

- Full ashtrays
- Matches within reach of young children
- Electrical appliances plugged in near sinks or tubs

■ Have a fire prevention campaign. Check your home to see if it has any of the fire hazards discussed here. Find out about other types of fire hazards too. Fireproof your home. Help your family install smoke detectors. Early warning can help save lives.

Fire Emergency Readiness

Planning ahead of time will help you to know exactly what to do in a fire emergency. Here are some guidelines:

If your clothes catch on fire:

1. Stop where you are.

2. Drop to the floor or ground. Do not run. If you run, the fire gets more oxygen and burns faster.

3. Cover your face with your hands.

4. Roll back and forth—or wrap a coat, blanket, or rug around you to smother the flames.

If another person's clothes catch on fire:

1. Get the person to drop to the ground.

2. Wrap a coat, blanket, or rug around the person to smother the flames, or roll her over and over.

If fire breaks out in your home:

1. Get yourself and other people out of the house as quickly as possible. Practice fire drills from different rooms, especially bedrooms.

2. Don't try to stay and put the fire out. Fires can spread *very* quickly.

3. Pull the nearest alarm box, or call the fire department from your neighbor's house. Give your name and address and the exact place of the fire. If you call from an alarm box, stay there to direct the fire truck when it arrives.

If smoke comes into a room and the door is closed:

1. Do not open the door.

2. Feel the door. If it is cool, open it a little and hold it with your foot. Feel the air outside with your hand. If the air is not hot, walk out of the house immediately. If the door is warm, block the crack under the door with a rug, pillows, or sheets. Go to the window and call for help. Stay near the window until help arrives.

If you wake up to find your bedroom full of smoke:

1. Roll out of the bed directly onto the floor.

2. Crawl to the nearest exit. Smoke rises, so the coolest, freshest air will be close to the floor. Remember not to open any door without first checking to see if it is warm.

If fire breaks out while you are in a public place:

1. Stay calm.

2. Walk quickly and quietly to the nearest exit.

3. Do not panic or run.

With your troop and with your family, talk about and practice what to do in case of fire.

■ Have a Stop, Drop, and Roll relay race. Here's how to play. Divide into two teams. Have each team form a line behind the starting line. Mark a line about 15 feet (4½ m) ahead of the starting line. At the signal "go," one girl from each team walks to the line, stops, drops, and rolls to her right and left two times. She returns to the end of the team line. The next girl does the same. The game continues until all members of one team finish.

■■ Role-play what to do when:
* You are home alone and a fire breaks out.
* Your younger brother is playing with matches.
* Your friend's clothing catches on fire.
* A pan on the stove catches on fire.

■■ Find out how a smoke detector works and where to place one in a home, troop meeting place, or other location. If your home does not have one, talk to your family about getting at least one.

■■■ Plan, talk about, and practice fire escape routes. Draw a fire escape plan for your home, troop meeting place, or school. Be sure to include a second escape route.
* Draw the floor plan.
* Label each room, all doors, and all exits.
* Label a place outdoors where the family or troop can meet.
* Place the floor plan in a spot where everyone can see it.
* Practice fire drills several times a year.

■■ Make a puzzle, word hunt, or other game to help others learn about fire safety.

■■■ Talk with a firefighter to learn more about his or her job and about ways of preventing fires.

■ Ask your fire department for free window stickers to place in rooms where children sleep so firefighters can find the rooms quickly in an emergency. Help give out the stickers in your community.

Fire Safety Tips to Remember
* Remove fire hazards.
* Never open a warm door. Use a second escape exit, such as a window.
* Do not go back for anything once you are safely out of a fire.
* Do not hide in a closet or under the bed during a fire.

- Stay low, crawl away from the smoke, and get out fast.
- Plan and practice fire drills.
- Place smoke detectors in your home.

Money Management

Do you get an allowance? Have you ever earned money babysitting or doing chores for someone? Have you ever gotten money as a gift? At one time or another, you have probably had some money of your own. And you made some decisions about what to do with it—whether to spend it, save it, donate it to a special cause. Making decisions about money is not always easy, but you will have to make more and more of these types of decisions as you grow older.

■■ When you make decisions about money, you become a money manager. The more you learn about ways to handle money, the better money manager you'll be. One way to start is by keeping track of all the money you spend in one week. Every time you pay money for something, write down the amount spent and what it was for.

Below, read about Lauren's experience with money management.

LAUREN'S MONEY

Lauren's neighbor, Mrs. Costa, was about to start a new job and needed someone to walk her two dogs every weekday morning and afternoon. She offered Lauren the job. Lauren couldn't believe her luck. Living next door would make it easy. Besides, Lauren could do it without giving up any of her after-school activities.

The $15 she would get each week sounded terrific, and Lauren's answer was an instant yes. The newest record albums, that blue dress she'd seen in the store, horseback riding lessons . . . Lauren's mind was swirling with all the things she could get. Suddenly, her mother interrupted her thoughts: "Lauren, this is a good time for you to open a bank account and start saving for college. You know that it'll be expensive, and we'll all have to work to make sure you can go." Lauren felt crushed. How could this be? Her spending money was gone before she had even earned it.

Lauren's Choices

Is there a way for Lauren to help save for her college education while still having some money to spend now?

Here are some choices for Lauren. Can you think of others?

1. Not say anything and just feel hurt.

2. Tell her mother her ideas for how the money could be used.

3. Get angry with her mother because she just doesn't understand.

Lauren was upset for a while, but finally decided that her mother was right. Maybe, though, something could be worked out. Lauren talked with her mother, and they agreed that some money could be saved and some could be spent now on things Lauren wanted.

Budgeting is deciding how to divide up money and when and how to spend or save it. How would you budget for Lauren over a one-month period? Think about how you would spend the money if it were yours.

At the end of several months, Lauren will have a bit more money than she put into the bank because the savings will have earned interest (money that you get from keeping your savings in a bank).

Try this activity:

■■ Set up your own budget. Try to follow it for at least two months. Figure out how much money you will probably have from allowance, gifts, and earnings. Then plan how much you will spend and how much you will save. Fixed expenses are those that are pretty similar from day to day. Flexible expenses can be adjusted. If you don't have enough money, you may have to do without one or more of these flexible items, which could include records, snacks, movies, or gifts.

See page 108 for a budget plan you could use.

Other Activities for Learning About Money

■■ These activities can help you learn more about money management:

- Learn how to write checks.
- Find out how to open a bank account.
- Make up a troop budget.
- Take part in a Girl Scout product sale.
- Invite an accountant or someone who works in a bank to come to a troop meeting and explain what she does.
- Help your family with a household budget.

Your budget plan might look something like this:

	Week 1		Week 2		Week 3	
Money I expect to have (total):	_____		_____		_____	
Fixed expenses:	Planned	Spent	Planned	Spent	Planned	**Spent**
School lunch	_____	_____	_____	_____	_____	_____
Bus money	_____	_____	_____	_____	_____	_____
Troop dues	_____	_____	_____	_____	_____	_____
Flexible expenses:	Planned	Spent	Planned	Spent	Planned	**Spent**
Snacks	_____	_____	_____	_____	_____	_____
Records	_____	_____	_____	_____	_____	_____
Movies	_____	_____	_____	_____	_____	_____
Savings:	Planned	Spent	Planned	Spent	Planned	**Spent**
For school	_____	_____	_____	_____	_____	_____
For personal use	_____	_____	_____	_____	_____	_____
Donations to charity:	Planned	Donated	Planned	Donated	Planned	**Donated**
	_____	_____	_____	_____	_____	_____

MANAGING MONEY FOR YOUR GIRL SCOUT ACTIVITIES

Whether you work on Girl Scout activities on your own or with a group of friends in a troop, you'll probably have some ideas for things to do that require money.

Troop Dues

Troop dues can be used to help you and your troop do all kinds of interesting projects and activities.

The members of the troop agree on an amount that can be afforded by all. They must decide:

- The amount (10¢, 20¢, 25¢, more?).
- When to collect the dues (every meeting, once a month?)
- Who will collect them (elected treasurer, leader?)
- A safe way to keep the dues (locked box, troop bank account?)
- How the dues will be used (special event, help someone else?).

For more about troop dues, see page 72.

Money management is more than dividing, saving, and spending. It's also learning what to buy, deciding on the best time to buy something, and deciding when to save. Knowing how to spend or invest money wisely is all part of being a good money manager and a smart consumer.

Earning Troop Money

Girl Scout troops often plan and carry out activities to earn money for the troop treasury. One way to raise money is through a Girl Scout cookie sale. Permission to carry out this activity, or some other activity to earn money, is important. Your Girl Scout leader needs to get permission from the local Girl Scout council, and you will need the permission of your parent or guardian. It is also important for everyone to know safety rules for the activity.

■■ When you participate in a money-earning project, you can learn a lot by including some of these activities:

- Learn about product advertising.
- Be able to explain how your product or service benefits consumers.
- Develop a budget showing how the money will be spent.
- Find out about businesses related to the money-earning activity.
- Explore careers related to the product or service.

YOU ARE A CONSUMER

Whether you buy things for yourself or help others decide what to buy, you are making decisions as a consumer. But what caused you to buy the item you did?

Consumer Awareness Activities

■■ COUPON CLIPPING Look through magazines and newspapers to find cents-off or money-back coupons. Cut out all that you find. Divide your

coupons into two piles. Make one pile for products that your family often uses. Put all the others in another pile. Which pile is bigger? Add up the money value of each stack. Use the coupons to help with the next household shopping trip. Give the coupons that your family can't use to others.

■■ COMMERCIAL LOG Find out how many commercials appear on TV and how you react to them. Using a watch with a second hand, make a log something like this:

Day 1		
Show	Local news	
Commercial	3D cola	Happy Time cereal
Time	30 secs.	60 secs.
Kept My Attention?	Yes	No
Made Me Want to Buy?	Yes	No

After you have done this, think about what made you want to buy something you saw. Talk to others about how you reacted to the various commercials.

■■ COMPARISON SHOP Select an item that you would like to buy, like a new pair of jeans. Go to several stores or look through catalogs. Find out if there are differences in price or quality. Thinking about everything you have learned, decide which you would buy. You can also do this with someone in your family, for an item that the family really plans to purchase. It can be anything from a new breakfast cereal to a large piece of furniture.

Tools for Living

Tools help people do things. Tools can be simple, like a pair of scissors, or complicated, like a power drill. Learning to use simple household tools can help you to deal effectively with many problems that arise. These skills also give you the opportunity to express yourself creatively.

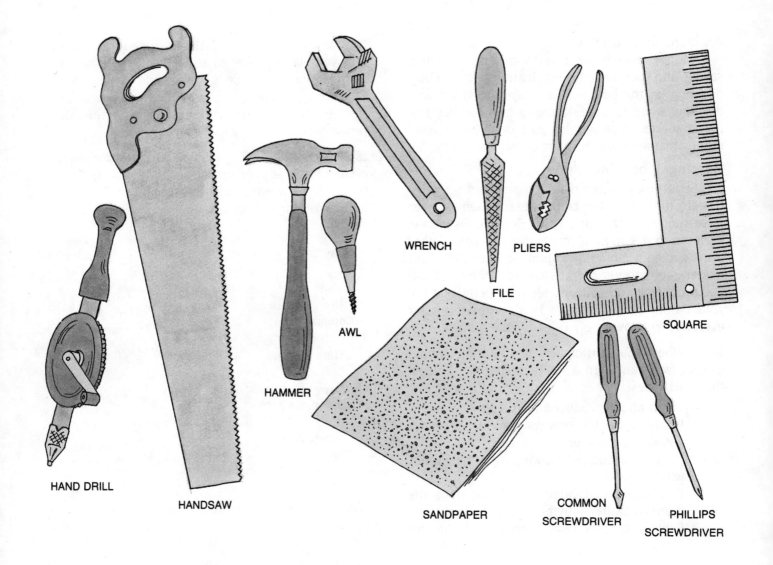

HAND DRILL

HANDSAW

HAMMER

AWL

WRENCH

PLIERS

FILE

SANDPAPER

SQUARE

COMMON
SCREWDRIVER

PHILLIPS
SCREWDRIVER

BASIC TOOLS

Review this list of basic tools. See if you can find one or more samples of each tool. Have someone show you how to use them properly and safely.

Hammer—for pounding and removing nails
Handsaw—for cutting wood
Common screwdriver—for putting in or removing common screws
Phillips screwdriver—for putting in or removing Phillips screws
Sandpaper—for smoothing rough surfaces
File—for grinding down or smoothing surfaces
Awl—for making holes
Pliers—for gripping things
Wrench—for turning nuts and bolts
Square—for helping to make right angles
Hand drill—for making deep holes

TIPS FOR TOOL SAFETY

1. Always make certain you have completely learned how to use a tool before you start working with it.

2. Never use power tools unless you have an adult working with you.

3. Make sure you have a clear working surface.

4. Keep tools out of the reach of young children.

5. Don't use broken or poorly maintained tools.

6. Wear goggles to protect your eyes if there are chips, splinters, or sparks around.

One of the best ways to learn how to use tools is to make something. The project on page 111, making a catch board, will help you practice using some basic tools.

■■ CATCH BOARD This board can be used to hang keys, memo pads, glasses, jewelry, or anything else you want to have within easy reach.

You will need: a flat wooden board, at least 12 nails (each about 2 inches long), a hammer, medium-grain sandpaper, a small block of wood (about the size of a bar of soap), a paintbrush, pliers, a rag, heavy cord or string, a saw, paint or clear varnish, a drill (or 2 ring-topped screws).

Directions:

1. Use a saw to cut the board to measure 12 inches by 18 inches (30 cm by 45 cm).

2. Wrap the sandpaper around the small wood block, and smooth the edges and surface of the board.

3. Rub the board with a rag to remove the dust caused by the sanding.

4. Paint or varnish the board. You can:

Paint designs of different colors

Paste on pictures, drawings, or decorative pieces of paper and then coat with a clear varnish

Do line drawings with a permanent ink marker and then coat with a clear varnish.

5. Let your decorated board dry for at least 24 hours.

6. Hammer the nails ½ to 1 inch (1¼ to 2½ cm) deep in assorted places on the board. The nails can coordinate with your design. Whatever you want to keep on the board will hang from these nails.

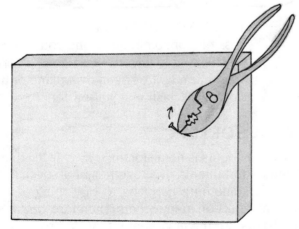

7. Grip the nail heads with a pair of pliers and bend each nail upward.

8. You can prepare the board for hanging in two different ways. Use method A if you have a drill for making holes; use method B if you do not.

A. Drill holes in the top corners of the board.
B. You will need two ring-topped screws for this hanging method. These screws will go on the top corners of the board. Start holes for the screws by using an awl or by gently hammering nails into the spots for the screws. Pull the nails out and put the screws into place. Turn them until they fit tightly. If turning becomes difficult, insert a screwdriver through the opening and turn.

9. Thread the cord through the holes (or rings) and then knot the ends so that the cord will not pull through.

Outdoor Adventures

Wherever you live, the out-of-doors can offer you many adventures. Some outdoor experiences are simple, like discovering unusual plants in a small park or vacant lot. Other experiences involve a great deal of planning, like a camping trip lasting days. Whatever you decide to do, it makes sense to always:

Plan ahead.   Walk softly.
Dress right.   Learn skills.
Keep safe.

PLAN AHEAD

Whatever activities you wish to do in the out-of-doors, they will turn out most successfully if you plan ahead. The amount of planning necessary will depend on the activities you have in mind and the amount of experience you have. You will need to decide what to do, where to go, and what types of food, clothing, and equipment will be needed. You also will need to learn more about the particular outdoor activity, find out about special safety needs, and make a kaper chart.

DRESS RIGHT

Wearing the right clothes for your outdoor activity is very important. Some activities are actually dangerous if you are not dressed right. Your clothing can protect you from things like poison ivy, thorny bushes, or a very bad sunburn. Of course, you will need to dress to stay warm in cold weather and cool in hot weather. The proper shoes and socks can make an exploratory hike comfortable and safe. They can prevent blisters and make walking easier.

KEEP SAFE

■ ■ Safety rules are important for everyone to know. Learn the basic rules first and then the special ones for longer trips. See pages 93–97 for safety rules everyone should know.

Some outdoor safety tips are:

- Learn about poisonous plants and animals that you should be careful to avoid.
- Learn about the symptoms and first aid treatment for hypothermia (low body temperature) and heat exhaustion (high body temperature). See page 101.

- Be prepared for weather emergencies. Know what to do when there are storms, lightning, flash floods, sudden drops in temperature, high winds, or tornadoes.
- Never leave the group. Always stay close by.
- Stay found. If you become lost or separated from your group, remember these rules:

   STOP. Don't keep walking, as that could make it very hard for rescuers to find you.

   CALM DOWN. Don't panic.

   THINK. Try to figure out where you are and how you can make yourself as safe as possible.

   SETTLE DOWN. Find a dry spot for resting. Protect yourself, but make sure that rescuers will be able to find you. If you are sheltered, leave at least two signals that can be seen by others.

ATTRACT ATTENTION. Make it as easy as possible for someone to find you—blow a whistle, sing loudly, make a sign in an open area that might be seen by a plane or helicopter, or flash a signal mirror.

WALK SOFTLY

The out-of-doors is home for millions of living things. Plants and animals live together in a special balance. If something happens to one thing, it may have an effect on many others. Therefore, be careful not to disturb the environment. Always try to leave a place in the same condition as you found it, or even in better condition.

LEARN SKILLS

The skills you'll need will probably vary from one outdoor trip to another. Here are some basics.

◼️ ◻️ Knot Tying

Follow the directions here to learn the important skill of knot tying.

Knot	Use	Directions
Overhand	When only a simple knot is needed	
Square	To join two cords of the same thickness	
Half hitch	To fasten rope around a ring	
Clove hitch	To fasten one end of a rope to a tree or post	
Sheepshank	To shorten rope	

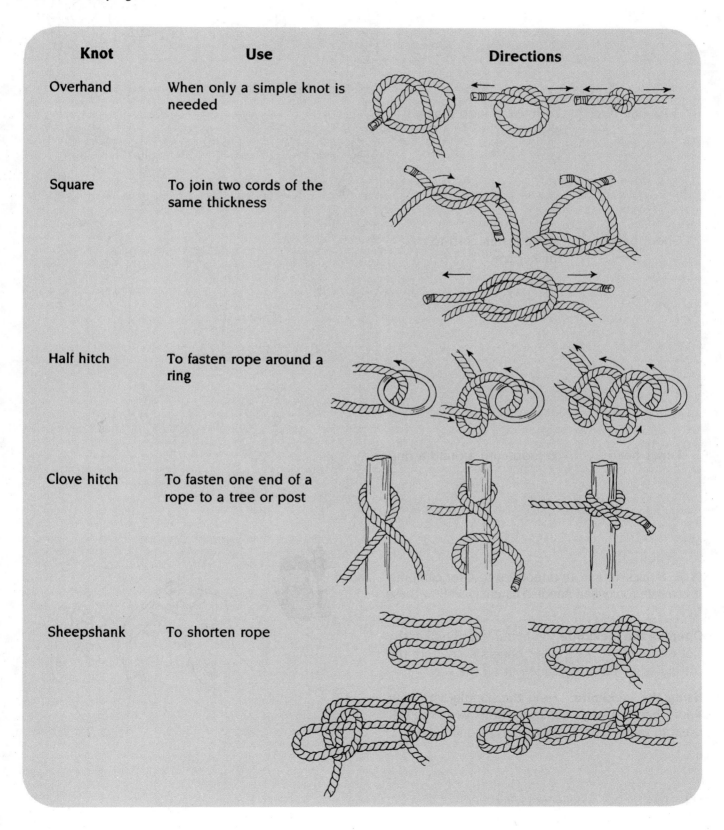

Knot	Use	Directions
Bowline	To make a loop that won't slip	
Taut line hitch	To make a loop that will slip	
Sheet bend	To tie a thin cord to a thicker cord	
Lark's head	To loop cord around a ring	

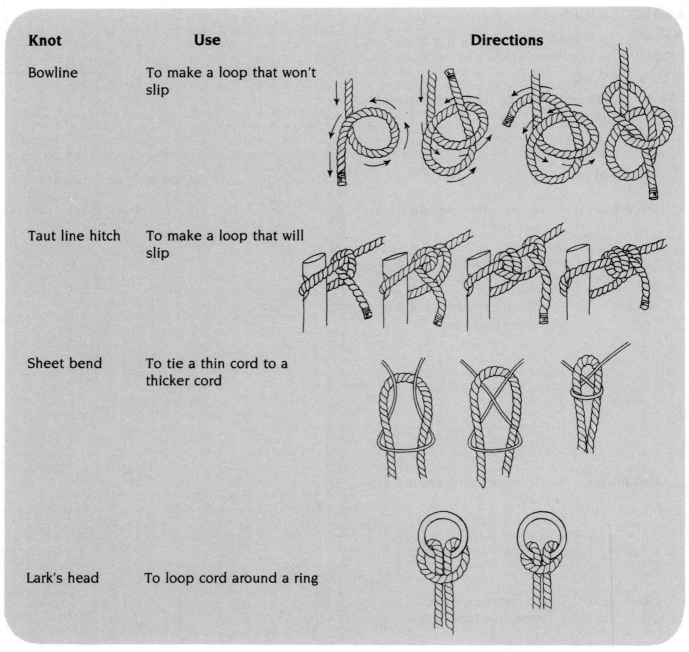

The Jackknife

■ ■ A jackknife is an important tool for camping. It is a safe tool when handled carefully. Follow these tips.

Opening the jackknife Put your thumbnail in the slot of the blade. Keep your fingers away from the cutting edge. Pull the blade out all the way.

Using the jackknife Hold the handle with your whole hand. Always cut away from you. Keep at least an arm's length away from anyone else.

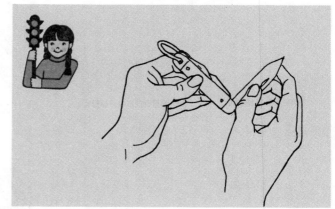

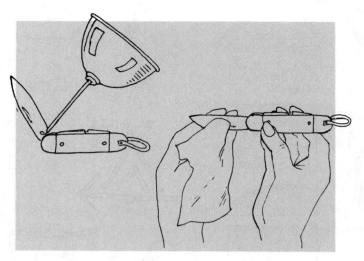

Cleaning the jackknife Keep your knife clean and dry. To clean, hold the cloth at the back of the blade, away from the cutting edge. Wipe carefully across the whole blade. Oil the hinge with machine oil. Never clean the blade by rubbing it in dirt or sand. This dulls the blade and makes the knife hard to open and close.

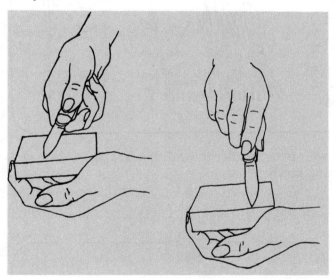

Sharpening the jackknife A sharp knife is safer and more useful than a dull one. Keep your jackknife sharp with a sharpening stone (called a carborundum stone). Hold the stone in one hand and the open jackknife in the other. Keep the fingers that are holding the stone below the top edge of the sharpening stone. Lay the flat side of the knife blade on the flat surface of the stone. Keep the knife blade almost flat. Move the blade over the sharpening stone in one long motion.

Turn the blade over and sharpen the other side by pulling the blade back in one long motion.

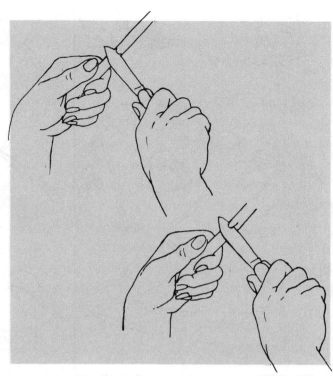

Whittling a point Shape a stick by cutting off little chips of wood, one at a time. Do not try to cut off big pieces. Cut slowly so your knife will not slip.

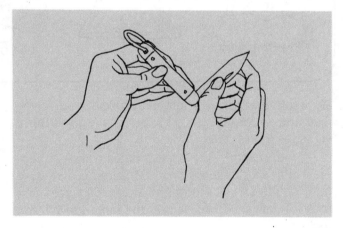

Passing the jackknife If you are going to pass a jackknife to another person, close it first. If you are using some type of knife that cannot be closed, such as a paring knife, grasp the blade along the dull edge and pass the handle to the other person. This way you have control of the sharp edge of the knife. Always say "thank you" when you have received a knife. This is a signal that you are holding the knife safely.

Finding Your Way in the Out-of-Doors
See page 116 for some ways to tell directions and avoid becoming lost.

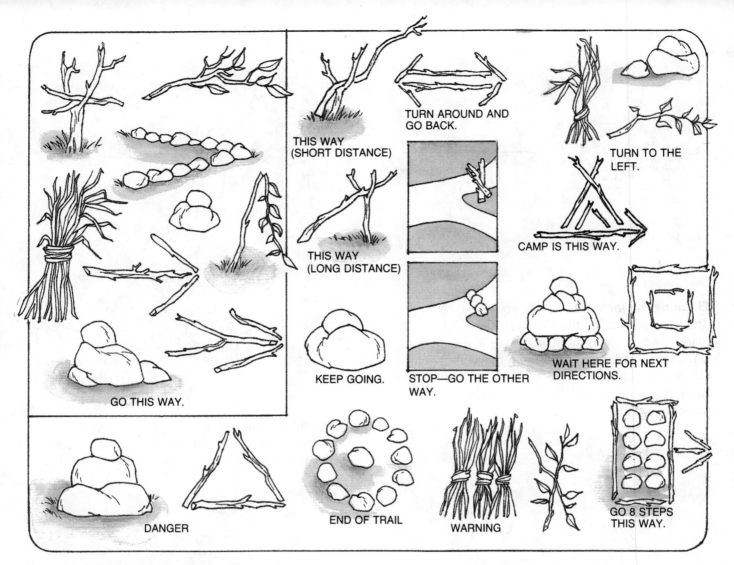

THIS WAY
(SHORT DISTANCE)

TURN AROUND AND
GO BACK.

TURN TO THE
LEFT.

THIS WAY
(LONG DISTANCE)

CAMP IS THIS WAY.

KEEP GOING.

STOP—GO THE OTHER
WAY.

WAIT HERE FOR NEXT
DIRECTIONS.

GO THIS WAY.

DANGER

END OF TRAIL

WARNING

GO 8 STEPS
THIS WAY.

▨ **Trail markers** There are special trail signs (see above) for hikers. Girl Scouts have used these signs for many years.

Notes can also be used to lay a trail that people will use for a day or two. For example, a starting note could say, "Go straight ahead 50 paces and look for your next note under the large grayish-tan rock."

You can make up and agree upon your own trail sign language. Just be sure that you remember all safety rules and have an adult to help you.

▨ Practice laying different kinds of trails.

▨▨ **Directions in the sky** The sun or stars can also be used to find directions. In the morning, the sun is in the east. If you stand with your left shoulder toward the sun, you will be facing south. In the afternoon, the sun is in the west. If you stand with

your left shoulder toward the sun, you will be facing north.

Whenever you are facing north, the east is to your right, west is to your left, and south is behind

you. At night, Polaris, the North Star, can be used to help you find north. The easiest way to find Polaris is to first find the Big Dipper. See the diagram.

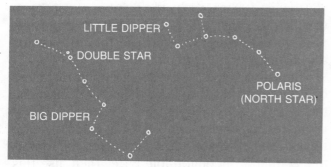

Finding directions with a compass

A compass has a small, magnetized needle that turns easily. Because the earth is like a giant magnet, the needle will turn to point to the magnetic north of the earth. When you know which direction is north, you can find all the other directions.

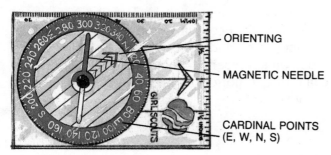

ORIENTING

MAGNETIC NEEDLE

CARDINAL POINTS (E, W, N, S)

The letters on a compass are N for north, E for east, S for south, and W for west. To find north from where you are standing, hold the compass flat in your hand. Turn the compass housing until N lines up with the direction-of-travel arrow. Then turn yourself around until the red end of the needle lines up with N. You are now facing north.

The numbers on a compass represent the 360 degrees of a circle. The sign for degree is °. East is the same as 90° on the compass face. West is 270°. What would 180° be?

Mapping directions

One way to show people how to get from one place to another is to use a map. There are many kinds of maps. Some maps are very detailed, while others just show a few features of the land. Some maps are even developed from photographs taken by orbiting satellites.

A simple sketch map is a type you can make easily. Whether your map is of a rural area or of city streets, you will need to have a **legend**—a list of what all the symbols on the map mean. Here are some types of things that are often shown in a legend.

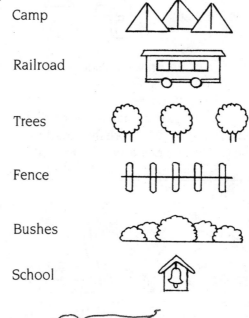

Camp

Railroad

Trees

Fence

Bushes

School

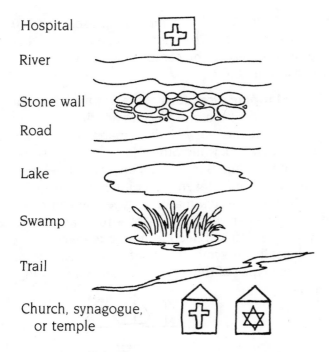

Hospital

River

Stone wall

Road

Lake

Swamp

Trail

Church, synagogue,
or temple

A sketch map can be drawn **to scale**—that is, to give an idea of distances. For example, 1 cm = 20 paces or 1 inch = 35 paces.

Make your own sketch map showing distances and a legend. You can find more information about mapmaking in *Outdoor Education in Girl Scouting.*

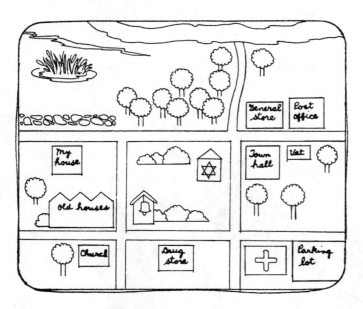

■ ■ **Measuring distances**   Knowing your pace is a good way to measure distances. A pace is two steps. Mark off a distance of 330 feet (100 meters) on the ground. Walk it five times, counting the number of paces it takes each time. Try to walk naturally each time. (Always start the walk with your

toe at one end of the measured distance.) Is the number of paces about the same each time? When you have decided what is a natural-length pace for you, divide 100 meters by the number of paces you usually take. That will give you the length of one pace. In the future, you can use this to measure any distance on the ground.

It is also helpful to be able to judge distances by how long it takes to walk them. Mark off a distance of ½ mile. (Or instead, you might walk 1 kilometer, which is about ⅔ of a mile.) Practice timing yourself to see how long it takes you to walk the ½ mile at a comfortable pace. Then, use this knowledge later to roughly judge distances you have covered according to how much time the walk has taken.

Preparing for Tomorrow

As you grow older, you'll be learning even more skills for living. Becoming more responsible for how you look, feel, and act can help you enjoy things today while preparing you for making your dreams come true tomorrow. More about that in the next chapter.

CHAPTER 8

Hopes and Dreams

As the three 11-year-old girls walked home from school one afternoon, one of them, Sherry, turned to the other two and asked, "What do you want to be when you grow up?" "We're too young to think about that now," Laurie answered. Then she quickly changed the topic. "Let's meet at the playground after we finish our homework." Laurie's discussion of afternoon plans was interrupted by Ann, who said, "I think now is a good time to start asking ourselves questions about our future. I think I'd like to be a lawyer like my Aunt Ingrid. But I also want to get married and have a family." Laurie obviously wasn't interested in talking about the future. "Race you to the stop sign," she said as she started to run.

Is it too early for Sherry, Laurie, and Ann to be discussing their hopes and dreams for the future? Probably not. Discussing, dreaming, planning, thinking, searching, questioning can happen

right now for you. This doesn't mean that you have to know what you want to be or that you have to make any definite decisions at your age. But there are many ways that you can start today to prepare for exciting possibilities tomorrow. This chapter offers some ways for you to explore your hopes and dreams.

Daydreaming

■ Do you daydream? You may sometimes daydream when you're supposed to be concentrating on something else. Perhaps people have told you that daydreaming is a waste of time. At times it is—but daydreaming can also be an important way to begin to explore your future. And it's something you can do alone—any time and any place. Give yourself a few minutes now to daydream about:

- What you'll look like in 5 years, 10 years, 15 years
- What form of education you might pursue (for example, will you go to vocational school? college? medical school?)
- Where you will live in 10 or 20 years (the same place where you are now? far away?)
- How you could make the world a better place if anything were possible
- What you'll be doing for fun when you get older (skiing? painting? flying to exotic places?)

- What you would do if you suddenly received a million dollars
- What kind of work you'll be doing when you finish school (you can daydream about several different possibilities)

Your daydreams are very personal. They might be shared with a few other people, perhaps your closest friends. Or they could be kept completely private—for your thoughts only. They don't have to be realistic at all—just allow your imagination to fly free.

Do the daydreaming exercise at different times. You might want to keep a diary of the different daydreams to see how they change as your life changes.

What Else Can You Do Now?

Many sections of this handbook give you opportunities to find out more about yourself. Look at the material on:

- Leadership (pages 65–73)
- Talents (page 29)
- Decision-making (pages 55–64)
- Values (pages 25–28)
- Hobbies (pages 30–31)

Learning about yourself now can help you to figure out what kind of person you might want to be like

in the future. Below, read about three girls who are roughly your age. How do their abilities and interests shape the goals that they have now?

SANDRA'S STORY

Sandra is gifted in many ways. She consistently receives top grades in her class. A poster she made for a contest on safety won first prize. She is also very popular. Her classmates recently elected her to be the president of their fifth-grade class, and she is a patrol leader in her Junior Girl Scout troop. Sandra enjoys experimenting with the chemistry set that her parents gave her for her birthday. She's an excellent swimmer and has just joined her school's swimming team. Sandra dreams of becoming a scientist someday, maybe even winning the Nobel Prize. Or maybe she'll become a member of the United States Olympic swimming team. Or perhaps she'll devote herself to the arts while at the same time raising a family. She might even become President of the United States. Because she is so good at so many things, Sandra will someday have to make choices. And that can be very hard to do.

KATHERINE'S STORY

Eleven-year-old Katherine sings every chance she gets—on the way to school, in the shower, cleaning her room—but always out of tune. All the practice

in the world will never make her a singer. Unfortunately, a singing career is what Katherine is dreaming of. Katherine's singing teacher doesn't have the heart to tell her that she isn't talented. So Katherine persists in her unrealistic hope of one day becoming a professional singer. If only Katherine would realize that she should start dreaming of a different career. Perhaps she could develop her natural gracefulness and pursue dance lessons. Or maybe she could become a writer or journalist. She's already shown some talent in that area (receiving grades of A on all of her school writing assignments, even when she doesn't try very hard).

MARIA'S STORY

At twelve, Maria is the oldest of the five children in her family. From the time Maria was seven, she was taking care of the younger brothers and sisters. For some, this might be a chore, but for Maria, it was mostly fun. Maria is not only great with the children in her family, she seems to have an extraordinary ability to relate to any child she meets. She is remarkably patient and has a warm sense of humor. Maria has a lot of friends with whom she plays softball, basketball, and other games. She's not particularly good in sports, but she always has fun playing. As a student, Maria is probably just a little better than average. But she is well-liked by her teachers and classmates. Maria's fondest dream is to become a kindergarten teacher. She under-

Hopes and Dreams for Now

It might be interesting to see what happens when you set a goal that can be fulfilled in a few weeks or months. The goal could be related to school—such as getting higher grades in a particular subject. It could be related to Girl Scouting—maybe completing a badge that you began months ago or starting a service project. Getting along better with a member of your family could be a goal. So could finding a friend to share your new interest in computers.

PLANNING TO REACH A GOAL

In the space below, write down a specific goal.

_____

_____

_____

_____

_____

stands who she is and what she is good at. Her very special talents will probably allow her to fulfill her dream.

■ Alone, or with a group, make up some other stories like the ones you just read. In each case, figure out whether the dreams match the girl's interests and abilities. If you're doing this with a group, one girl can start a story and others can continue it.

Planning carefully can greatly help a person to achieve a goal. Below, describe the steps that you plan to follow to accomplish your goal. Figure out the dates by which each step will be completed.

Steps to Reach My Goal	Planned Date of Completion for Each Step
_____	_____
_____	_____
_____	_____
_____	_____
_____	_____

I plan to reach my goal by _____ .

Often others may be able to help you fulfill your dream. Write down the names of those people below.

People Who Can Help Me	How?
_____	_____
_____	_____
_____	_____
_____	_____
_____	_____

On the date that you thought your goal would be reached, fill out the checklist below.

	YES	NO
1. My goal has been reached.	___	___

If you answered yes to question 1, go to question number 6.

If you answered no to question 1, answer questions 2, 3, 4, 5, and 6.

	YES	NO
2. I am no longer interested in the goal.	___	___
3. I did not put enough effort into fulfilling my dream.	___	___
4. The steps I outlined were not right for me. I need to change the steps and try again.	___	___
5. I am still working on my goal.	___	___
6. I am happy with what I did to reach my goal.	___	___

If you did not achieve your goal or are unhappy with the results, you can:

- Continue working toward your goal using the steps that you already outlined.
- Figure out new steps that may be more useful

- Find other people to help you
- Substitute another dream and start all over

Plans for the Future— School

Why are you in school right now? To develop new skills? To learn information? To learn ways of getting along with your peers and with adults? School will continue to be important in the future for those reasons and others.

At some point, you'll have to make some decisions about the direction of your education. Remember the daydreaming activity from page 121? What type of education were you thinking of? The type of education you pursue will depend on many things.

- What you want to learn
- What you want to do as a career
- Other responsibilities you may have that could prevent you from continuing in school (like a family or a job).

Many different types of education are available to you. To find out about them, you and others who are interested can:

- Interview students or graduates from different types of schools.

- Visit different schools and talk to the teachers and students you meet there.
- Read about various forms of education (for example, you might find a book in the library about the experiences of a student in business school).
- Request, by letter or by telephone, information about the programs in various schools.

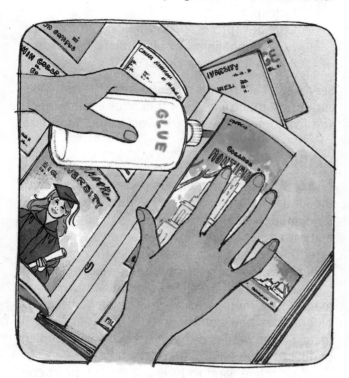

■■ You might keep a scrapbook of the information and materials you've collected. Keep adding to it as you come across new material. This scrapbook can be a valuable reference for you in years to come.

■■ You can also get insights into the importance of education by interviewing adults who did not have the opportunity to get the kind of education they wanted.

The Best Job For You ✓

Women have more job opportunities today than ever before. But choosing a career can be one of the most difficult things you will ever do. You will be using everything you know about yourself—your interests and abilities, likes and dislikes—to make a decision. Here are some activities to get you started on the exciting path of career exploration.

CAREER AND INTEREST/TALENT CARDS

■ With a group, write down the names of different careers, each on a separate index card. Try to get as many as possible—perhaps 50 or 100. Include some that are unusual (like a tour guide in Indonesia) and others that are not typically held by women (engineer is one example). On other index cards, write an interest (for example, enjoys working with people) or talent (for instance, great at math). Again, write as many of these as possible. Now, try to match the interest/talent cards with the career choices. Several interest/talent cards can apply to the same career.

■ For fun, without looking, select one career card and one interest/talent card. Tell a story about the person with that combination. Imagine the possibilities. You might get some funny combinations, like a mechanic who values cleanliness above everything, or a computer programmer who loves working with animals.

OBSERVING THE MEDIA

■ Look at how women are shown on television (both regular programs and commercials) and in the movies. What kinds of roles do they usually play? How are their roles different from those played by men? Discuss these questions in your troop or with some other group of friends.

HOBBIES AND CLUBS

■ ■ ■ ■ ▫ A fun way to explore jobs is by starting a hobby or joining a club related to a career possibility. See pages 30–31 for information about hobbies. If you want to be an actress, you can join a dramatic club or put on amateur productions with your friends. If you're interested in computers, you can join a computer group. If you're interested in a career in fashion design, you can do some sketching or start collecting magazine photos of interesting outfits.

CAREER EXHIBIT

■ ■ ■ ■ ▫ With a group, set up an exhibit to show different types of careers. The group can paint, make collages, sculpt figures of workers, and write stories or poems that tell about various aspects of the work. For instance, one project might compare the uniforms, hours, salaries, and amount of people contact in three different jobs (perhaps a carpenter, school principal, and real estate agent). One girl should act as exhibit coordinator to make sure that a large number of occupations are being represented.

GUEST SPEAKERS

■ ■ ■ ■ ▫ Invite people who work at interesting jobs to visit your troop or group to talk about their work. They might be able to show how they work (for instance, a photographer could demonstrate picture-taking techniques) or they might bring in a product they have made at work (for example, a chef could bring in some pastries or bread she has baked). A panel representing different careers could be organized. Panelists might be asked to speak about what they like and don't like about their work and about the special skills or education needed for their jobs.

TRIPS TO WORKPLACES

■ ■ ■ ■ ▫ Visits to work environments can be exciting and informative. These are just a few of the places and people you might visit:

- Museum (curators, guides, researchers, guards)
- Department store (buyers, cashiers, sales people, designers, window dressers, managers)
- Hospital (doctors, nurses, orderlies, administrators, scientists, technicians, therapists, dieticians)
- Television station (performers, directors, makeup artists, costume designers, writers, producers, technicians, lawyers)
- Newspaper offices (reporters, editors, clerks, typesetters, accountants, managers, secretaries)
- College (professors, administrators, business managers, public relations people, counselors, researchers).

See pages 157–161 for more information and ideas about possible trips. Add other work environments and list some of the workers you would find there.

ROLE MODELS

■ ■ ■ ■ ▫ Role models are people who are doing the kinds of jobs you might be interested in later. Role models can be important sources of information and inspiration. For example, a girl interested in a career in science can learn a great deal about it from a woman who is a researcher.

You can read about role models in books and magazines. There are probably many interesting biographies and autobiographies in your local library. Fiction stories can also describe what it might be like to have a particular career.

You might want to have even more direct contact with a role model by interviewing one. Ask what attracted her to her career, what she likes most about her work, what she doesn't like about her job, what kinds of people she works with, what an average day is like.

If you can get permission, "shadow" (follow) a role model through a full workday. What does her workplace look like? What different types of work does she do? Does she usually work alone or with other people? What hours does she work?

Because you're exploring at this point, you might want to shadow several different people who have different kinds of jobs.

FAMILY CAREER TREE

■ ■ ■ ■ ▫ Involve your family in your career exploration. Find out the kinds of work your parents, grandparents, cousins, brothers, sisters, aunts, and uncles have done or are doing. Some of your relatives may have hobbies in which they use skills that could be turned into a paying job (for example, sewing skills might be used in a dress designing career). Find out about these types of skills as well.

Set up a family career tree like the one below.

SET UP A BUSINESS

■■ Learn about the excitement, fun, and hard work that come with being in business. You might conduct a garage sale, write and sell a newspaper, plant and sell flowers, write and sell computer programs, or produce a play and invite friends, neighbors, and relatives to buy tickets to see it.

When you decide to close your business, think about what you learned, what you enjoyed, and what you disliked about the experience. Maybe another time you can start a different venture.

Putting It All Together

At different times in your life, different things will be important. What works at one time may not work at another time. What works for one person may not work for another. Finding the right combination of career, leisure-time, and family activities will add to your happiness.

■ Part of the fun and challenge of growing up is being able to make decisions and to change when needed. The puzzles below show a variety of ways to put the pieces of your life together. Put together a puzzle to represent your life now and another one to represent what you hope and dream it will be like when you've grown up.

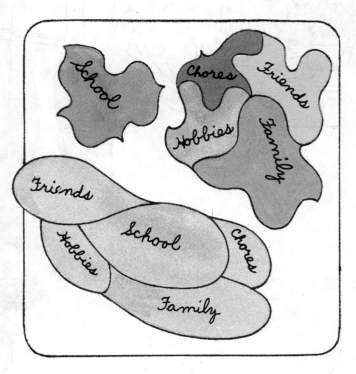

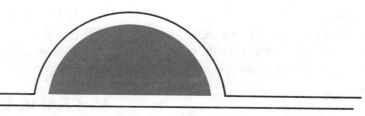

CHAPTER 9

Creative Explorations

Everyone can be creative. You don't have to be a great artist or composer. Just use some imagination to explore the world from your home to the great outdoors!

This chapter will show you many ways to be creative—from going on trips to enjoying music, from organizing your things to making up games.

Making Your Surroundings Unique

Everyone needs a place where she can feel at home. You may feel especially comfortable in your room or in a certain part of your family's home.

Your room or your surroundings show that *you* live there. The books you read, things you've made, collections and special pictures you have, or plants you're growing all show something about you. Your space is unique—just like you!

There are many ways you can decorate your surroundings to help you feel they are your own. Try some of the following activities.

GROW SOMETHING FOR YOUR SPACE

■ Plants help keep your surroundings fresh by adding more oxygen into the air and are pleasing to the eye.

Some people believe that a plant grows best when you talk to it. Others have found that plants do well when soft, classical music is played for them. You can find out about the mysteries of plant life for yourself by growing a green plant friend for your space.

Plants from Cuttings

■ A cutting is a small piece of a plant that is cut off to grow into another plant. Ivy, violets, geraniums, and coleus are good plants to grow from cuttings.

What to do:

1. Cut off a piece of a fully grown plant just below the place where the leaves join the stem.

2. Place the cutting in water until roots start to grow. When there are many roots, place the cutting in a plant pot that has good drainage and healthy soil.

3. Keep the soil damp until the plant has formed strong roots. Give the plant lots of sun.

DECORATED CONTAINERS

■ Jars, boxes, cans, and candy or cookie tins make good storage containers for things you collect. Decorate and label your containers with paint, crayons, markers, or colorful paper. You might try spreading a thin layer of glue on some containers and then placing sand, shells, beads, or pebbles on the glue to make a pretty design. Protect your design with varnish.

WASTEBASKET WONDER

■ Change a plain wastebasket into a Wastebasket Wonder!

1. Pick out one of the colors in your room and paint the inside of the wastebasket that color.

2. Cover the outside with fancy paper, a map, or drawings.

3. Carefully spray or paint the outside with varnish to protect your design.

MACRAMÉ WALL HANGING

■ Macramé is the art of tying knot patterns to make decorative and useful objects. There are many kinds of macramé knots. You can design a wall hanging of your own by learning a few of them.

You will need: 8 pieces of heavy string or cord (each at least 4 feet, or 1.2 m, long), a thin stick or rod (at least 12 inches, or 30 cm, long), and scissors.

1. Fold each piece of string or cord in half. Bring the ends up, around the stick, and through the cord loop to tie each cord onto the stick. This knot is a half hitch. (You will have 16 pieces of string hanging down from the stick, and you can begin to make square knots.)

2. To make a square knot, use four cords. Bring the first cord on the right over the next two.

3. Place the fourth cord over the first cord and under the two middle cords. Pull it through the space between the first and second cords.

4. Pull the ends of the first and fourth cords to tighten the knot. You now have half of a square knot.

5. Bring the cord that is now in the fourth position back over the two middle cords.

6. Place the cord in the first position over the fourth cord and under the two middle cords. Pull it through the space between the third and fourth cords.

7. Tighten the knot. You now have 1 square knot.

8. Make 3 more square knots with the other cord pieces by repeating steps 2 through 7. Use the next 4 cords along the stick to make each new square knot.

9. You can create your own design pattern with square knots. Here are some ideas you might try:

- Switch the cords you use to make the knots.

- Make a long string of knots with the same cords, then switch cords.

- Make a string of half square knots. (To do this, repeat steps 2 through 4.) You will create a spiral pattern.
- Leave spaces between knots.

- Double the number of cords you use, so as to make a large square knot.

- String beads along the cords between the knots.

Macramé Finishing Tips

When you have completed your pattern, some cord ends will be longer than others. Make them even by cutting away the extra pieces.

To keep cord ends from unraveling, tie a triple overhand knot and trim the ends.

SHARING IDEAS

To learn additional ways to organize and decorate your surroundings, find other girls who are interested in the subject. Together you can:

■ Invite an interior designer or architect to speak to your group.

■ Visit each other's homes and see how each girl uses and decorates her surroundings.

■ Look through magazines, books, and store catalogs for ideas.

■ Look at some of the arrangements and model rooms in a large department or furniture/home design store.

DREAM LIVING SPACE

■ Since you won't be able to immediately carry out everything you might want to do with your surroundings, start keeping ideas and materials in a scrapbook.

Include pictures, drawings, photographs, notes of designs, and organizing and decorating ideas for your dream living space. Then one day, when you have the time, space, and money, you will be ready to make your dream surroundings become real!

MORE ACTIVITIES

Try some of the badges in *Girl Scout Badges and Signs* that are related to this topic. They include Architecture, Art in the Home, Art in the Round, and Art to Wear.

Sports

Playing sports, either alone or with others, is a great way to have fun. No matter which sport you choose to play, you will need to learn certain skills and follow certain rules. Be a good sport—play fairly and try to do your best.

TIPS FOR PLAYING SPORTS

- Always do warm-up exercises before taking part in a sports activity (see pages 38–40), and always do cool-down exercises afterwards (see pages 40–41).

- Wear clothing and shoes that are comfortable and suitable for the sport you are playing.

- Use equipment that is in good condition.

- Play in a safe area that is free of hazards.

- Drink water when you need to.

- Stop playing when you get hurt or feel tired.

Individual Sports Word Find

T	U	F	R	I	S	B	E	E	G
U	J	G	O	T	W	S	Z	N	Y
M	B	O	W	L	I	N	G	E	M
B	A	R	G	N	M	D	G	O	N
L	T	S	N	G	M	N	P	X	A
I	Z	E	G	N	I	T	A	K	S
N	T	O	B	L	N	N	U	V	T
G	R	N	C	C	G	W	G	I	I
E	U	Y	R	Y	S	N	P	O	C
E	C	V	F	L	O	G	M	Y	S

INDIVIDUAL SPORTS

Individual sports are those which can be played alone or with one partner. How many individual sports can you think of? (Note that these are different from team sports like basketball.)

■ ▪ See how many individual sports you can locate in the Word Find above. The words may be written horizontally, vertically, or on the diagonal.

A word may read from left to right ("badminton") or from right to left ("notnimdab").

Here are some of the words to look for:

cycling	skating
swimming	tumbling
golf	tennis

Besides these, there are four other sports in the Word Find.

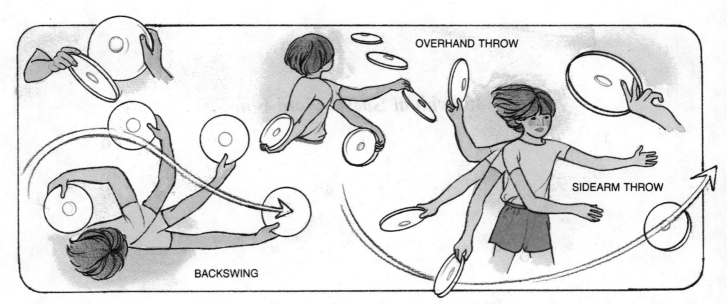

OVERHAND THROW

SIDEARM THROW

BACKSWING

Frisbee

■ Frisbee is an individual sport played with a plastic flying disc that is tossed back and forth. It is easy and fun to play and it's great exercise.

Frisbee was developed by inventor Fred Morrison after World War II. He started playing with pie tins and then turned to plastic discs because they flew better.

Try some of these activities with a Frisbee:

1. Practice holding a Frisbee. Place your thumb on top and your index finger under the rim.

2. Practice throwing a Frisbee. Try these methods:

BACKSWING. Stand sideways with the Frisbee in your hand. Turn your wrist and forearm in toward your body. Then unwind your arm with an easy motion.

OVERHAND THROW. Grip the Frisbee with your thumb underneath and with your other four fingers on top. Face forward and turn your wrist and forearm behind your back. Bring the Frisbee forward quickly. Keep your arm straight and even with your shoulders.

SIDEARM THROW. Hold the Frisbee with your thumb on top and two fingers on the bottom. Swing your arm down and throw.

3. Play a game of Frisbee with a friend. Stand 15 or 20 yards (14 or 18 meters) apart and take turns throwing. You may throw and catch with the same hand, or throw with one hand and catch with the other. When the Frisbee is caught, the catcher

gets one point. Make up any other rules you wish and decide how many points it takes to win.

In one variation of the game, if the catcher tries her best and cannot reach the Frisbee, she still scores a point. If the catcher could have reached the Frisbee and misses it, the thrower scores a point.

For more individual sports activities, see the Individual Sports badge in *Girl Scout Badges and Signs*.

STUNTS AND TUMBLING

■ Stunts and tumbling are gymnastic activities that help you develop strength, flexibility, balance, and coordination. Safety is very important when doing these activities. To help you do them safely and correctly, a spotter must be present. The spotter would be an adult or older girl who has had special training in gymnastics. You will need to work on a mat. Wear shorts and a T-shirt or leotards and tights. You may do these activities in your bare feet.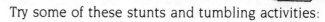

Try some of these stunts and tumbling activities:

■ SEAT BALANCE Sit on the floor. Hold your ankles in front of you with your elbows inside your knees. Place your feet flat on the floor and bend your knees. Raise your legs so that your knees are straight with your toes pointed. Balance on your buttocks (seat) for five seconds.

■ SEAL SLAP Lie face down with your hands under your shoulders. Push off from your hands

SEAL SLAP

SEAT BALANCE

PARTNER STUNT

and toes so that you can clap your hands in the air before touching the mat.

■ PARTNER STUNT Pick a partner. Lie face down on the floor with heads together and feet in opposite directions. Place a basketball or volleyball with some of the air taken out of it between your heads. Together, try to stand up and return to your starting position without dropping the ball. Do not touch the ball with your hands.

GROUP SPORTS

■■ Some sports are played by a group of people. The players are sometimes divided into opposing teams. Double dutch and group juggling are two group sports you might like to try.

Double Dutch

More than 300 years ago, the British came to New Amsterdam (now called New York City) and saw Dutch children jumping with two ropes. They named the game "double dutch."

You will need two ropes, each at least 12 feet (4 m) long, and three or more girls to play.

Turning double dutch Two girls turn a pair of ropes in an eggbeater motion. To start, each girl holds the end of a rope in each hand. Turn each rope in a circle, one after the other. Use the left hand to turn one rope clockwise and the right hand to turn the other rope counterclockwise. When one rope hits the floor, the other should be high in the air. Turn until you get a steady beat. You might sing or say rhymes to keep the beat.

Jumping double dutch Stand close to the side of one of the rope turners. When one rope clicks the floor, this is your signal to jump in. Jump in without touching the ropes. Once you jump in, stand with your arms held at your sides and your elbows bent, or arms bent with hands clasped at your stomach. Don't look down or lean forward. Lift your legs one after the other. Your feet should be raised at least four inches (10 cm) off the ground so you will have room for the ropes to go under. Try to land on the balls of your feet. When you have finished jumping, leave the ropes quickly without touching them.

After you have practiced a while, you might want to form teams and have a double dutch contest.

Group Juggling

Juggling is a sport in which you do tricks with balls or other objects. You try to keep more than one ball in the air at the same time.

For group juggling, you will need three or more balls of the same size (tennis balls are good to use) and five or six people.

Stand in a circle with everyone facing the middle. One person starts by throwing the ball to another person. The person catching the ball passes it to a third person. This continues until everyone has tossed and caught the ball once. Each person should drop her hands when she has had a turn. The last catcher tosses the ball back to the first person. Practice this a few times.

Once you are comfortable with one ball, start two balls going around the circle in the same direction at the same time. Then, add a third ball. Each person may call out the name of the person she is tossing the ball to. If a ball drops, pick it up and continue the pattern.

To make the game even more fun, add more balls or start one ball in one direction and another ball in the opposite direction.

TEAM SPORTS

■ Team sports are played with two groups of people who compete or match their skills against each other. The team members must work together to do their best. Remember that the important thing is to have fun! Some team sports are basketball, field hockey, lacrosse, soccer, softball, and volleyball.

Basketball

Basketball is a team sport played with a ball and basket, usually on a court. It was invented in 1891 by James Naismith and first played in Springfield, Massachusetts. Basketball is a fast game that involves a lot of running, dribbling (bouncing the ball while moving), passing, and shooting.

Learn and practice these skills:

- Dribble a ball while running, starting, and stopping.
- Pass a ball to another player in these ways: with two hands, over the head, and from a bounce.
- Shoot a ball into a basket in these ways: with two hands, with one hand, and from a jump.
- Guard a player who has the ball.

Regulation basketball is played on a court that has one basket at each end. The two teams are made up of five players each. Points are scored by throwing the ball into the other team's basket. A team gets two points for every successful basket shot. But, if a player has violated a rule (like tripping a player), the other team is given a foul shot. A foul shot is made from the free throw line. One point is earned for a successful throw.

Players move the ball by dribbling it or passing it to members of their team. Walking or running with the ball without dribbling it is not allowed.

You can learn a great deal about the specific rules and strategies by watching a game—live or on television.

If you don't have ten players or a regulation court—or if you want to try something different—you can play variations of the game. For example, you can:

- Play a game with two, three, or four players on a team.
- Play with only one hoop.
- Change the rules so that only passing is allowed—no dribbling.
- Use a wastepaper basket on the ground as a hoop and play "wastepaper basketball"!

If you are interested in other team sports, try completing the Group Sports badge in *Girl Scouts Badges and Signs.*

SPORTS EQUIPMENT

Making sports equipment can be fun and easy. Some types of equipment can be made from things that would normally be thrown away. Things like newspaper, yarn, cloth, coat hangers, and plastic cups might be used.

■ ■ ☐   A nylon stocking racket is one piece of equipment you can make. You will need a wire coat hanger, one leg of stocking hose, masking tape, and scissors.

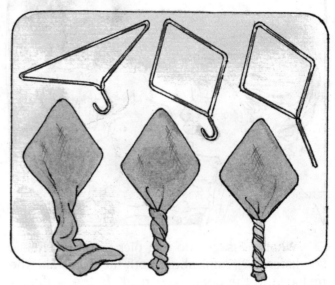

Bend the hanger into a diamond shape. Bend the hook of the hanger to form a handle. Slowly, pull the foot of the hose over the hanger down to the handle. Wrap the leg of the hose around the handle. Tape the hose to the handle. Cut off any extra hose. You now have a lightweight racket. You can use it to hit a badminton "birdie" or a ball made of foam or sponge. Make another racket and have fun with a friend.

Other ideas for sports activities:

- Have a tournament.
- Plan a family sports day.
- Have relay races.
- Learn to twirl a baton.
- Join a sports club.
- Take lessons in your favorite sport.
- Try to design and make your own piece of sports equipment. Create a game in which it is used, and play the game with some friends.

Whatever sport you participate in, remember to play fair, play safe, and have lots of fun!

Expressing Yourself Through Art

Everyone can create art. The creation may be a drawing, a musical piece, or even a special meal—anything that adds beauty or pleasure to the world. Art is also used to express feelings about life and to send messages to people.

What messages do you pick up in the music you listen to? (Think about both the words and the melody.) in the poetry you read? in the sculpture you see? Whether you create it or observe it, art is meant to be enjoyed. Different people may react differently to a particular piece of art. A painting that you think is beautiful may be nothing special to a friend. Art can teach you about how others see the world around you, and can help you to better understand yourself and your feelings.

THE VISUAL ARTS

Paintings, photographs, and sculptures are examples of the visual arts. Visual art can be hung on a wall or displayed in some other way so that you and others can enjoy it.

A Color Picture

■ The use of colors is very important in the visual arts. Colors can carry messages about feelings or mood, time of day, season of the year, and distance. Create some pictures with colors.

You will need: paints, markers, crayons, or pencils in an assortment of colors.

Ideas for pictures:

- An abstract that shows your mood or feelings without using real people or objects
- A picture that looks as realistic as you can make it
- Pictures of the same subject done with very different colors
- Pictures of the same scene during different times of the day or year
- Two pictures of the same scene—one a close-up, the other from a distance

Mural Painting

■ Murals are pictures painted on walls. They usually tell a story in a series of scenes, and are sometimes done by a group of artists. You may not be able to paint directly on a wall, but you can make a mural using a long roll of white paper. You can design the mural with your family or with your Junior Girl Scout friends. Cover the floor with newspapers. Stretch your mural paper on top of them. Decide what the design of your mural will be. You can combine words or slogans with your pictures. Each person can be responsible for a different section of the paper.

Printmaking

■ Using a small block of wax, carve a design to use for printing.

You will need: wax, a cutting tool or knife, water-based printing ink (or water-based paint), a cookie sheet or glass baking dish, and blank cards or paper.

Here is how to make a printing block:

1. Smooth the surface of the wax by covering it with aluminum foil and ironing it with a warm iron.

2. Draw your design on the wax.

3. Carve the design with your cutting tool or knife.

4. Pour the ink onto a cookie sheet or baking dish.

5. Dip the printing block into the ink.

6. Press the wet printing block against a card or paper to make a print.

Make as many prints of your design as you want. If ink gets into the carved-out areas, rinse the sculpture in water, dry it, and put more ink on the block.

The rinds of cantaloupes, pumpkins, oranges, and dried corn cobs—as well as sponges—make interesting prints that have grainy textures. Can you think of anything else you could use to make prints? Perhaps you and your friends could collect a variety of items, then have a printing party where you make stationery and cards.

Paper-Mache

■ Paper-mache can be used to make a great variety of things—from three-dimensional art forms to masks and stage scenery. It is a material easily and inexpensively made. Here are two recipes.

You will need: paper (newspaper, paper towels, paper egg cartons), paste (flour and water or white glue mixed with water), and a bowl for mixing.

To make a flour paste, mix one-fourth cup of hot water to one-half cup flour. To make white glue paste, mix 2 tablespoons of water to 1 tablespoon of white glue.

PAPER PULP METHOD

1. Shred the paper into very small pieces. Make at least 3 cups of paper bits.

2. Put the paper bits in a mixing bowl.

3. Soak in about 3 cups of hot water for at least one-half hour.

4. Drain water and then squeeze paper pulp so it is not dripping wet.

5. Mix with paste so that paper-mache is moist but not dripping.

6. Use a hand or electric beater to make a smoother, less lumpy pulp.

PAPER STRIP METHOD

1. Tear newspaper into strips about 1 inch (2 cm) wide.

2. Dip strips into paste.

Forming with paper-mache Mold like clay, or shape pulp or wrap strips over other forms: wire frames, bottles, cardboard containers, wads of newspaper, blown-up balloons. You can make sculptures, drama props, masks, toys, decorative items for your room. After the paper-mache has dried, it can be painted and varnished.

Photography

■■ Photography can be your way of showing other people how you see the world. If a dozen people took pictures of the same thing, each picture would be different. A good photographer is a good observer who pays attention to details. A facial expression, the patterns in a series of buildings, contrasts of light and dark, the patterns of clouds—details like these never go unnoticed.

Some general guidelines for photographing are:

1. Keep your fingers off the lens to avoid leaving prints that can spoil your picture.

2. If you use a fixed-focus camera, stand no closer than four or five feet from your subject.

3. If your camera has an adjustable lens, focus the lens to get a clear image in the viewfinder.

4. To make sure your picture is clear rather than blurred, hold the camera still by keeping your elbows close to your body, and press the release button gently.

5. To make sure your pictures are straight rather than lopsided, hold the camera level when you shoot.

6. Learn to frame your photographs. While looking through the viewfinder, shift your position around until the scene looks exactly the way you want it to.

Choosing a subject to photograph   Some of the best pictures are planned in advance and have a specific purpose. The following activities will help you develop your photographic skills.

1. Take pictures of trees, houses, or buildings. See how many types, sizes, and shapes you can find. Take the pictures on different days in different outdoor light: bright and sunny, bright and partly cloudy, overcast.

2. Pick a shape and go around town photographing everything you find which has that shape or which contains that shape in it. The shape should be the focus—the center—of your pictures. Use common shapes easily found, like circles, squares, or rectangles.

3. Think about how you want to compose some pictures. Plan the background and the position of your subject. Also plan different angles for taking the photographs. For example, for a family portrait, will the family sit on the sofa in their home or relax on the grass in a park? In your picture of the lake, will you include the sailboat or only the swimmers? Take several well-planned pictures.

4. Use photographs to tell a story, with no words used. For example, the story might be about a school field trip, a family vacation, or a party. Take pictures from beginning to end. The pictures by themselves should tell the complete story.

Embroidery

■ Embroidery is a decorative design made in fabric with needlework. You can do embroidery on practically any firm fabric. Your jeans might look good with a picture of an animal or a rainbow stitched on them. Or you might want to decorate pillows, wall hangings, or stuffed fabric animals.

On some scrap fabric, try the basic stitches that are explained on page 141. Once you know a few simple stitches, making a picture or design with them is easy.

Decide what you want to stitch. Then draw your design with a pencil on paper to get an idea of what the completed design will look like. Choose a fabric that is easy to work with—not too stiff and not too flimsy. Cotton, wool, or linen would be fine. The paper design can serve as the pattern for your actual design on the fabric. To transfer the design, place tracing paper on top of the fabric with the dull side facing up. Now, place the paper design on top of the tracing paper and trace the design with a pencil or tracing wheel. (Tracing paper and tracing wheels can be found at stores that sell sewing supplies.)

Here are some tips on embroidery:

- Choose a needle with an eye large enough for your yarn.
- Use an embroidery hoop to hold the fabric tight, making stitching easier (but you can also work without a hoop).
- Make a plan for working with different types of stitches and different-colored yarns. For example, you might complete all the stitches in red before going on to green. Or you may decide to do all the chain stitches before starting the satin stitch.
- Pull the stitches to make them lie smooth. If you pull too hard, the fabric will pucker; if you don't pull hard enough, the stitches will be loose and untidy.

Running stitch   You can make straight or curved lines with this simple stitch. Bring the needle up through the material at point A, down at B, up at C, down at D, up at E, down at F. Continue stitching until your line is the length you want.

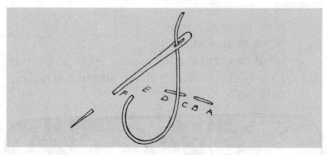

Stem stitch   The stem stitch is often used to outline shapes. You can also sew several rows of stem stitches close together to fill in an outlined shape.

Bring the needle up through the fabric at A and down at B. Then bring the needle up on the left, halfway between where you first came out and last went in. Make another stitch by pushing the

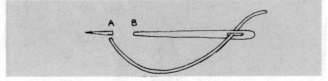

needle down, just slightly to the right of where the last stitch went in.

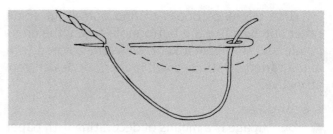

Repeat this. Keep the thread on the same side of the needle at all times.

Satin stitch   The satin stitch is good for filling in a shape. First outline the shape to be stitched with a running stitch or a stem stitch. Begin at one end of the shape. Bring the needle up at A and down at B. Bring the needle up again at point C, right next to A, and then down at D, right next to B. Repeat these steps until you have completely covered the area with the satin stitch.

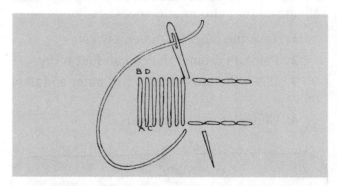

Chain stitch   The chain stitch is good for outlining shapes. Bring the needle up through the fabric at A. Make a loop with the thread and hold it down with your thumb. Insert the needle into the same hole you just came out of. Bring the needle up through the fabric on the inside of the loop at point B. Make another loop and insert the needle down again at point B. Come up now at point C inside the second loop. Repeat these steps until the shape is covered.

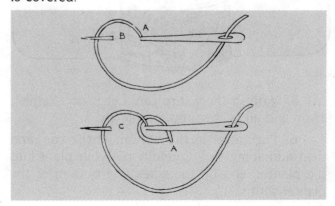

Use reference books to find out about some other stitches, like the buttonhole stitch, the cross stitch, and the French knot. Different-colored yarn and a variety of stitches will make your design very attractive.

Decoupage

■ Decoupage is a means of decorating with paper cutouts. Originally, decoupage artists cut out paper designs and glued them to furniture. When the furniture was varnished or lacquered, it looked as if the designs had been painted on.

You can use pictures cut out from magazines, postcards, greeting cards, wrapping paper, or photographs for decorating with this technique.

Decoupage for a planter You will need: a clean soup can, paint, a paintbrush, a cup of water, paper towels, pictures or decal stickers, varnish, potting soil, gravel (or pebbles and seeds).

1. Take the label off the empty can.

2. Paint all around the can and let it dry.

3. Clean the brush with warm water and then dry it.

4. Glue pictures on the can.

5. Varnish the entire can. Let it dry. Varnish again and allow it to dry completely.

6. Put gravel in the bottom of the can, and then add some soil. Carefully put your plant into the planter, and fill the sides and bottom of the planter with soil.

Fancy Paper

■ ■ In Japan, rice paper is made from a rice plant. This paper is very thin and delicate. To make your own fancy, delicate paper that looks something like Japanese rice paper, you will need: flower petals, small leaves, very thin twigs in interesting shapes, one-half cup of white glue, 2 tablespoons of water, white bonded typing paper, tissue paper.

To make fancy paper, follow these steps:

1. Arrange the flower petals, leaves, and twigs on the typing paper.

2. Mix the glue and water.

3. Place the tissue paper over the flower, leaf, and twig arrangement.

4. Completely cover the tissue paper with the glue solution. (It will be lumpy.)

5. Let the "rice paper" dry.

THE LITERARY ARTS

Poetry, plays, novels, and essays are some of the literary arts you can enjoy. You can read the works of others as well as write your own material.

Stimulate Your Imagination

■ See how many ways you can describe a woman crossing the street.

- How does she look?
- What is she wearing?
- What mood is she in? Is she happy, sad, tired?
- How is she walking? Is she limping, skipping, running?

- What kind of street is it? Is it wide, narrow, paved, a dirt road?

■ Describe a scene in nature. Make the reader see, hear, smell, taste, or feel the scene. Create a mood of joy, sadness, or fear.

■ Write a play, poem, or story. Here are a few ideas:

- A computer that produces its answers in poetry form.
- A girl who could see far away by looking into a special telescope.
- The first community of earthlings on Mars.
- Any original idea you may have!

Read the play, poem, or story to somebody. Ask the person what mood seems to be suggested by the piece.

THE PERFORMING ARTS

Performing arts are those which can be performed in front of an audience. Examples are dance, music, and play production.

Play Production

A play depends on the work of a number of people with a variety of skills, talents, and interests. Each person has to work in harmony with the others for the play to be successful. These are some of the members of a production group:

DIRECTOR. Directs the performances of the actors.

ACTORS. Perform on stage; must memorize lines and speak clearly.

PRODUCER. Organizes tasks.

STAGE MANAGER. Coordinates the backstage

area, scenery, and props; gives cues (signals) to actors.

SCENE DESIGNER. Decides how scenes should be designed or furnished and what props are necessary.

CARPENTER. Builds the props.

ARTIST. Draws or paints scenery.

COSTUME DESIGNER. Decides what should be worn.

MAKEUP ARTIST. Puts makeup on actors.

SOUND TECHNICIAN. Is responsible for sound effects.

PROMPTER. Helps actors who forget their lines.

PUBLICITY DIRECTOR. Makes posters and handles all publicity.

Of course, one person can have more than one job, especially in a small performance.

■ A play production is a good activity for getting all of your friends involved. Each person's job is important.

In order to help your show run smoothly, your production plan should include:

1. A list of backstage jobs that need to be done and the names of the people assigned to do them.

2. A time schedule for tryouts and rehearsals. How many? How long will each of them last?

3. A performance date based on the best estimate of when everyone will be ready.

Music and Dance

Music is a good way to bring people close together. You can begin or end your Girl Scout meetings and ceremonies with songs. Use these Girl Scout songbooks to select songs you will enjoy: *Sing Together*, *Girl Scout Pocket Songbook*, *Our Chalet Song Book*, and *Canciones de Nuestra Cabaña* (Songs of Our Cabaña).

■ Make up short stories or tales that you can perform by combining acting, dance, and music. Perhaps a small chorus could sing or play background music to help tell the story.

Here are some story ideas:

1. Magic shoes that enable the person wearing them to walk into the future or past

2. A special celebration of something that happened hundreds of years ago

3. A group stranded on a desert island

■ ■ **Folk music and dance** People all over the world have expressed their creativity through songs, dances, and drama. Here are some activities to help you get the feel of a culture through these arts.

- Listen to recordings or performances of folk music from around the world.

- Attend an ethnic arts festival that features performances of either traditional or new ethnic music.
- Learn a folk dance from another culture. Find out a little about the culture and share this information with someone else.

Science and Math in Action

Have you ever noticed the following?

- A rainbow forms in the sky after a spring rain.
- A bicycle left outside will start to rust.
- An opened bottle of soda pop left overnight loses its fizz.

The spark for science and math is a search for the what, why, and how of things. The best part is that this doesn't have to mean working in a laboratory or figuring out long, complicated formulas. In fact, science and math are everywhere and you can be a scientist in action!

WATCH AND WONDER

■ Watching the world around you can be exciting. Try this science scavenger hunt.

Try to find the things listed in the chart below. Put a check in the box next to each one as you find it. Then look closely at it—a magnifying glass would be helpful. The "What, Why, or How" column has some information about the things you are looking for.

Look for:	What, Why, or How
☐ A greenish-blue metal statue, light post, or building sign	Copper metal reacts with oxygen in the air, and a greenish-blue tarnish forms on the surface of the metal.
☐ A bird's feather	Feathers protect birds. If you gently pull apart the feather barbs, you can see how they connect.
☐ A rock with layers	Some rocks were formed from layers of mud, silt, or sand that hardened millions of years ago.
☐ A rainbow pattern of light	Sunlight, or white light, is actually made up of a combination of many colors. When white light passes through certain clear things (like a prism, raindrop, or bubble), it can be broken up into different colors.
☐ Steam	Heat can turn liquid water into a gas (steam).

SEE AND TELL

■ ■ Here is another science scavenger list. Try to find the things on this list and write your own "What, Why, or How" statements.

Look for:	What, Why, or How
A potato with sprouting eyes	_____ _____
A magnet	_____ _____
A leaf that's not green	_____ _____
A liquid with bubbles	_____ _____
Frost	_____ _____
Something that glows	_____ _____
Crystals	_____ _____
Signs of pollution	_____ _____ _____

WATCH CAREFULLY

Try each of these quick and easy activities, and watch what happens.

- **Eye changes** Try this with a friend. Take turns cupping your hand over one open eye for a minute or so, and then quickly pulling it away. You'll see how the pupil, the dark center of the eye, reacts to light.
- **Plants "drink" water** Cut the bottom end off a stalk of celery and put it into a glass of water colored with red or blue food coloring.
- **Moist air plus iron = rust** Put an iron nail or piece of steel wool in a dish of water. The water should partly (but not completely) cover the nail or steel wool. Check what happens two days later.
- **Mushroom spores** Take off the cap of a mushroom and put it down on a piece of white paper. Leave it for two to three days.
- **Air takes up space** Stuff a tissue into a glass. Hold the glass upside down and put it straight down into a sink of water. Pull it straight up. Try again, this time holding the glass sideways.
- **Surface tension** Using a fork, carefully lay a paper clip flat on the surface of water in a bowl. Then add several drops of dishwashing detergent.
- **Crystal formations** Fill two glass jars with water. Stir five tablespoons of epsom salts into each jar. Wet a piece of heavy cotton string. Put one end in each jar and let the center of the string drop over a small, clean plate. Check the plate every two days.
- **Probability** Flip a coin 10, 25, 50, or 100 times. Keep track of how many times it falls heads and tails.
- **Math in nature** Find each of these math shapes in nature: circle, square, hexagon, spiral, diamond, triangle, ellipse (oval).

PUZZLERS

Wanting to know answers to puzzling questions has started many scientists on their way. By thinking about problems, you too can make some good guesses about answers. Try these puzzlers. (After you've finished, turn to pages 148–149 for the solutions.)

■ RIDDLES

1. How can you throw a ball so that it always comes back?

2. Which weighs more, a pound of rocks or a pound of feathers?

3. A large, brown, feathered rooster on a rooftop lays an egg. Will it roll to the right or the left?

4. What is worse than finding a worm in an apple?

5. What is the difference between a new dime and an old penny?

6. When is a penny more than a dime?

■ THIRD ARROW   Can you add two straight lines to make a third arrow that is the same shape and size as the two in the drawing?

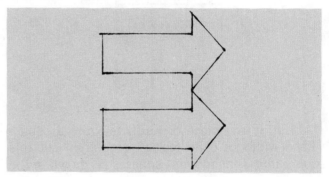

■ HOW MANY TRIANGLES?   See how many triangles you can find in this drawing.

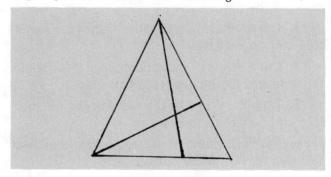

■ BUTTON THROUGH THE HOLE   Make this puzzle. Then try to solve it.

You will need: 1 thin strip of wood or heavy cardboard, 1 button, a piece of string 2 feet (61 cm) long.

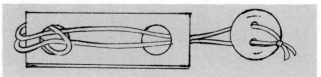

1. Cut a hole at each end of the wood or cardboard strip. Make sure the hole is smaller than the button.

2. Loop the string through the holes as shown in the diagram on page 147.

3. Pull the string ends through the button, and tie.

Now for the puzzle. Can you take the string off the strip without untying the button?

■ A COUNTING PUZZLE   Make this counting puzzle. Then scramble the numbers and put them back into the right order.

You will need: 2 pieces of cardboard, tape, marking pens, ruler, scissors.

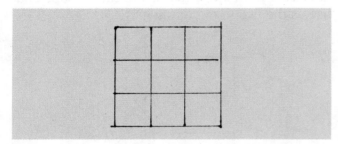

1. Cut one piece of cardboard into a square with a width of 6 inches (15 cm). Then cut this square into 2-inch (5 cm) squares as shown in the diagram.

2. Number the squares from 1 to 8. (You will not need the ninth square.)

3. Cut another square that measures 6½ inches (16½ cm) on each side.

4. Cut 4 strips of cardboard, each 2 inches (5 cm) wide and 6½ inches (16½ cm) long.

5. Tape the strips to the sides of the 6½ inch (16½ cm) square to form a box.

6. Put your number squares into the box so that they are not in the correct order.

Solve the puzzle by sliding one square at a time until the numbers are in order.

■ WRITE YOUR NAME   Can you write your name while tracing circles on the floor with your foot? Try it.

■ OPTICAL ILLUSIONS   Which horizontal line is longer?

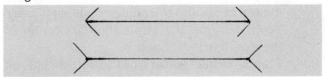

■ HEADS AND HEIGHT   How many times do you think you would have to wrap a string around your head to equal your height? Try it.

Answers to Puzzlers

Riddles

1. Straight up. Gravity will bring the ball back down to you.

2. They both weigh the same, one pound.

3. Neither; roosters don't lay eggs.

4. Finding half a worm in an apple.

5. Nine cents.

6. When you weigh them.

Third Arrow

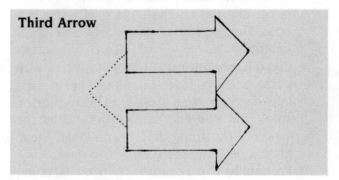

How Many Triangles?   Eight

Button Through the Hole

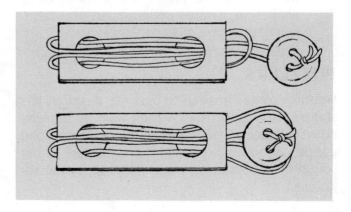

A Counting Puzzle There are hundreds of ways to slide the numbers into the right order. Keep trying.

Write Your Name The human brain has trouble coordinating two very different muscle activities. With practice you'll probably be able to do it.

Optical Illusions The horizontal lines are the same length. The lines at the end of the horizontal lines affect your judgment.

Heads and Height Most people find that they only end up wrapping the string around their head two or three times to equal their height. People usually guess a higher number of times.

DISCOVERIES

The answers to some science and math questions are easy to find. You might be able to look them up in a book or ask someone to tell you. But finding the answers by doing activities can be more exciting. Scientists often do many experiments before they make an important discovery. You can work toward some discoveries of your own, by doing the activities below.

Appearing Colors

■ You can make your eyes see colors that aren't there.

You will need: heavy white paper or cardboard, black India ink, a compass, a black felt-tip pen, scissors, a ruler, a hand mixer (or a record turntable).

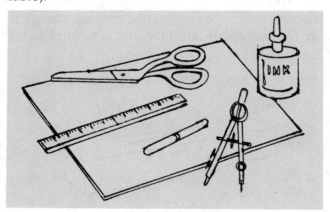

1. Use the compass to draw two 5-inch (13 cm.) circles on the paper or cardboard. Cut out the circles.

2. Draw a line through the middle of each circle.

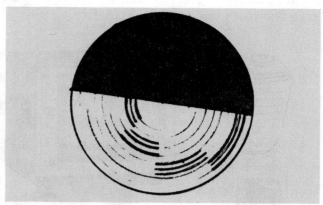

3. Color half of each circle black.

4. Use the compass to copy the other lines shown in the diagram. Keep making your compass smaller.

5. Darken the small lines with the felt-tip pen.

6. Punch a small hole in the middle of the circles, and tape the circles to one beater of the hand mixer (don't use the second beater). Or, if you are using a record turntable, stack the circles on the turntable after punching the holes.

7. Make the light in the room as bright as possible and start spinning the circle. Try different speeds.

The Discovery Your eyes will see very faint colors as each circle spins. Guess what? Scientists haven't discovered the full reason why this happens—they just know that it does.

Soda Pop

■ The noise you hear when a bottle or can of soda pop is opened is caused by gas bubbles escaping. You•can make your own soda pop.

You will need: lemonade (or limeade or orangeade), baking soda, a glass, a teaspoon.

1. Stir ½ teaspoon of baking soda into a glass of lemonade, limeade, or orangeade.

2. Watch what happens.

3. Taste the results.

The Discovery Baking soda and the water in the fruit drink start a chemical reaction that causes gas bubbles to form. These bubbles are not air. They are a gas called carbon dioxide. The same bubbles are in regular soda pop.

Technology Works for Us

From hair dryers to computers, technology is science and math working for you in exciting ways.

"I Can Live Without It"

■ Try this game with some friends. Divide into two groups. Each group decides on 15 technologies they would most want to keep. For example, your group might agree that they could live without an electric barbecue starter but they would definitely want a television. After each group has listed 15 items, they must make some new decisions. Now they must choose only 10 things, then finally the 5 they would most want to keep. Compare lists and talk about why particular things were chosen.

Computers

Computer technology does many things for us now and will be able to do even more in the future. Computers are like mechanical brains. People program computers to tell them what to do.

■ **Meet the computer** Ask someone to show you how a computer works. Try to follow the wire hookups to find out how the parts are connected. Find out about these parts:

Keyboard	Mouse	Printer
Disk drive	Monitor	Joystick

(Ask someone to point out these parts. Or find out about them by reading a magazine or book dealing with computers.)

■ **Think like a computer** Write out all the steps for doing something simple like eating, combing your hair, getting dressed, or fixing your favorite snack. Make a chart that shows the steps. Here's how:

1. Write questions in the diamonds.

2. Write information in the rectangles.

3. Write instructions in the parallelograms (slanted rectangles).

4. Connect these different shapes with lines and arrows.

To get an idea of how this is done, follow the Guessing Game chart on page 151.

Computer programmers call this type of diagram a flow chart.

Made by Me

You are used to buying many of the everyday things that you need, but you can make some of those things on your own. Try making the ones below.

■ COMPASS Compasses work because the earth is like a giant magnet. It is easy to make your own compass.

You will need: a strong magnet, a needle (one that will stick to the magnet), a cork big enough to lay the needle on, a thumbtack, a bowl of water, nail polish.

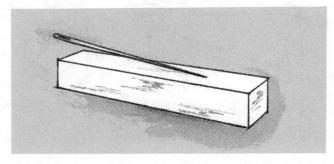

1. Stroke the needle along the magnet about 30 times in the same direction. The needle will be

STEPS IN A GUESSING GAME

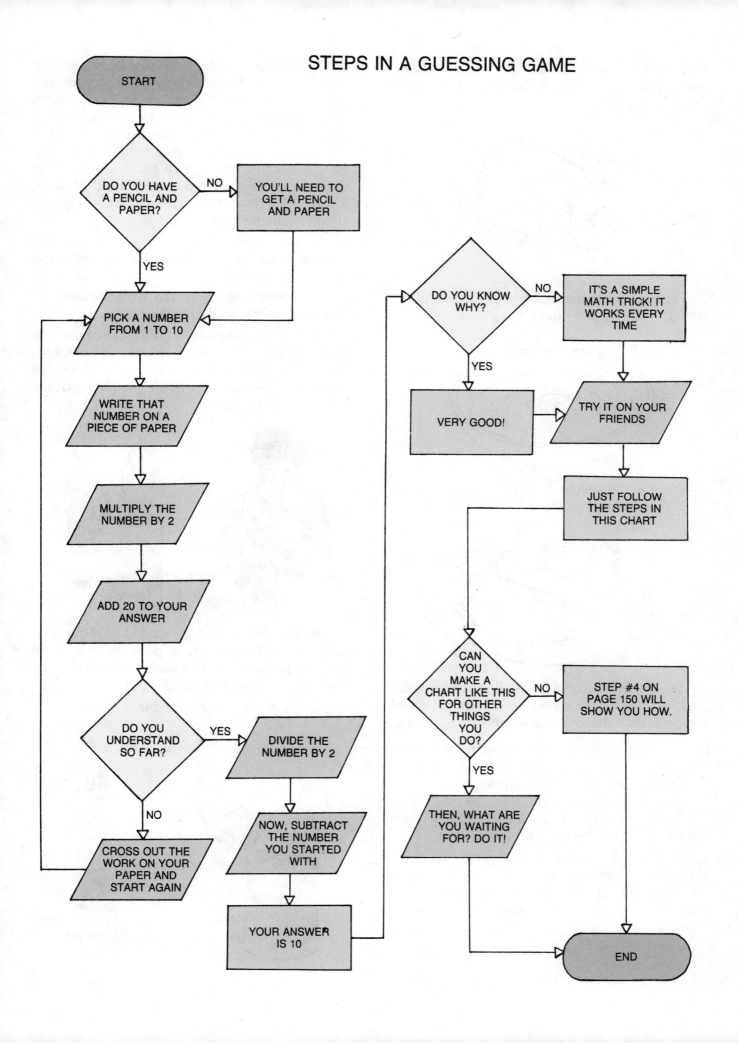

ready when it begins to act like a small magnet and can pull another needle toward it. Keep stroking until this happens.

2. Poke the thumbtack into the bottom of the cork. This will keep it from tipping over.

3. Lay the needle flat on the top of the cork. Then float the cork in the bowl of water.

4. The needle compass will line up in a north-south direction. Check your needle against a real compass. Put a dab of nail polish on the north end.

■ COPPER CLEANER   Put chemistry into action and clean up some tarnished copper. If you don't have any copper, try this on pennies.

You will need: a soft cloth, white vinegar, salt.

1. Stir 3 teaspoons of salt into ½ cup of white vinegar. Stir until the salt starts to dissolve.

2. Dip the cloth into the cleaning solution. Then rub the wet cloth on a copper item that is dark and tarnished. If the coating of tarnish is very thick, your solution may not work.

■ THERMOS BOTTLE   A thermos bottle can help keep liquids at the same temperature longer. Hot things cool down in cool air, and cool things warm up in warm air. So, if you protect your liquid from the air it will stay the same temperature longer.

You will need: a small glass bottle with a screw-on cap, a coffee can with a lid, small pieces of tissue paper (or shredded plastic, or bits of Styrofoam), strips of cloth 2 inches (5 cm) by 4 inches (10 cm), a butter knife.

1. Clean the bottle. If you want a decorated thermos, paint or paste things on the coffee can before you start.

2. Sprinkle some of the tissue, plastic, or Styrofoam in the bottom of the coffee can.

3. Put the bottle into the center of the can. Pack the rest of the tissue, plastic, or Styrofoam around the bottle all the way to the top to form an insulation. The top of the bottle should fit just under the lid of the can.

4. Lay the cloth strips on top of the insulation. Use the butter knife to poke the ends down between the sides of the can and bottle. This will keep your insulation from falling out.

5. Snap the coffee can lid into place.

Your thermos is now complete. Use a funnel to fill it. Compare how well your thermos works with how well an unprotected bottle works.

Progress in the Out-of-Doors

There are many ways to be creative when exploring the out-of-doors. Just as you must learn to add before you can multiply, it is important to learn some outdoor basics before you plan a long outdoor trip. Whatever you decide to do, remember to always plan ahead, dress right, keep safe, walk softly, and learn the necessary skills. See pages 111–118 in the "Day by Day—Skills for Living" chapter.

Follow the plan below to further build your outdoor knowledge and skills.

LOOK OUT

Begin to wonder what you might find outdoors. Try these starter outdoor activities:

- Make a list of outdoor places to visit.
- Learn about poisonous plants in your area.
- Make a list of animals that live in your area.
- Take different kinds of short hikes, such as:

  A COLOR HIKE. Find as many things as you can that are a particular color.

  A COIN HIKE. Flip a coin to decide your walking direction. Heads you go left 20 steps, tails you go right 20 steps. Try to make a new discovery at each coin flip.

  A ROCK HIKE. Look for different kinds of rocks.
- Look for signs of wildlife—footprints, nests, droppings.
- Find an area that you can protect and conserve.
- Set up an outdoor habitat indoors—aquarium, terrarium, ant farm, or worm farm.

MEET OUT

There are many special things to do in the out-of-doors and many indoor things that are more special when you can do them outside.

- Go on a senses hike. Look, listen, feel, and smell the out-of-doors.
- Sing songs on a hike.
- Take photographs of different outdoor settings.
- Paint a scene from nature.
- Make a bird feeder. Set up your feeder outside, and watch for the birds that come to visit.
- Take part in an outdoor game.

MOVE OUT

Practice your basic outdoor skills (see pages 111–118 in the "Day by Day—Skills for Living" chapter). Then visit an outdoor spot to put your skills into action.

- Earn a badge from the World of the Out-of-Doors.
- Write notes about your outdoor observations.
- Learn about the weather and what to do in weather emergencies.
- Plan and go on an outdoor trip that will last at least three hours.
- Carry out a conservation project.

EXPLORE OUT

Go on a special outdoor excursion that will last at least half a day.

- Prepare snacks or a meal for the outdoor adventure.
- Take a morning or afternoon trip; walking, biking, rowing.

- During the excursion, try earning a badge from the World of the Out-of-Doors.
- Have an ecology day.

Lou Henry Hoover Memorial Sanctuaries

Lou Henry Hoover Memorial Sanctuaries are the special places set up by Girl Scouts to protect plants and animals in their natural environment. These sites are given that name to honor Lou Henry Hoover, a woman who loved the out-of-doors and who at one time was the president of Girl Scouts of the U.S.A. and the wife of Herbert Hoover, the President of the United States from 1929 to 1933. As a part of her work with the Girl Scouts Movement, Mrs. Hoover shared her outdoor skills with thousands of other Girl Scouts. Think of ways you can continue to preserve the natural environment, just as Mrs. Hoover did many years ago.

COOK OUT

Prepare an entire meal in the out-of-doors. Whether you go on a camping trip or have a backyard cookout, you will need:

- A cool, dry place to store food
- A safe place to build a fire (or you could use an outdoor stove)
- An area to prepare food
- A place to eat
- A method for cleaning up
- A place to dispose of garbage or to store it until you can take it to a safe refuse area

Learn to make a vagabond stove and buddy burner for cooking in the out-of-doors. This set-up can be used to cook small portions of food for one or two girls. A vagabond stove is made from a large tin can. The buddy burner supplies the fuel used to heat the stove. You can cook on the lid of the stove or use a small frying pan to prepare meals for one person, like pancakes or fried eggs. A small kettle of water can also be heated on the stove.

How to Make a Vagabond Stove

You will need: a large coffee can, a metal cutter, work gloves, a punch can opener, wire, a nail, a hammer.

Follow these steps:

1. Wearing work gloves, use the tin snips to cut out a door about 3 inches square (7.5 cm square) on the side of the can near the open end.

2. Use the punch can opener to make three or four holes near the top of the can. Make sure the holes are on the opposite side of the can from the door.

3. Use the nail and hammer to punch two holes on opposite sides of the can.

4. Push the ends of the wire through the holes, and twist to make a handle.

Now, you have a vagabond stove! The open end of the can is the bottom; the air holes near the top serve as a chimney. The next thing you will need is a buddy burner.

VAGABOND STOVE

How to Make a Buddy Burner

■ You will need: 1 tuna fish or cat food can, a can lid, a coat hanger, wood chips or sawdust, wax (such as candle pieces), a pot of water, a large can (such as a coffee can).

Directions:

1. Put a small amount of the wax or candle pieces inside the large can. Set the can in the pot of water on the stove over low heat. Melt the wax. Be sure to do this step with an adult.

2. Spread the wood chips inside the smaller can. Make sure the chips are just below the top of the can. (Or, fill the can loosely with sawdust.)

3. Carefully pour the melted wax over the wood chips in the other can. Melt enough wax to fill the can almost to the top.

4. Make a damper—twist a piece of coat hanger around the can lid to form a handle.

Learn how to safely use the buddy burner and vagabond stove. Make sure an adult is present when you use them.

1. Find a level spot to set up the stove.

2. Light the top of the buddy burner with a match.

3. Wearing special work gloves or oven mitts, place the vagabond stove over the buddy burner.

4. Put out the fire by covering the buddy burner completely with its damper.

Learn these safety tips:

1. Make sure an adult helps you whenever you light a flame.

2. Always wear gloves. Melted wax is very hot, so never handle a buddy burner that is still warm. Wait until the wax is cool and hardened.

3. When the fire gets too hot, cover part of the burner with the damper.

4. When putting out the fire, completely cover the burner with the damper and leave it in place until cooled. OR, use work gloves to turn the vagabond stove upside down on top of the buddy burner and let it cool.

One buddy burner will last through several cookouts. After you have finished cooking, clean the top of the stove and cooking tins. The wire hanger makes the stove easy to carry.

■ Earn the Outdoor Cook badge described in *Girl Scout Badges and Signs.*

Some Outdoor Cooking Tips

1. Boiling water can be used to prepare many different things: hot cocoa, soup, instant rice, hard-boiled eggs, pasta (such as spaghetti), vegetables.

2. One-pot meals are easy to make and clean up after.

3. Store foods like meat and dairy products in a cool place to avoid spoilage.

4. Wrap ingredients and leftovers carefully.

5. Dry foods such as beef jerky, dried fruits, uncooked dried beans keep the longest.

For more information on cooking in the out-of-doors, see *Outdoor Education in Girl Scouting.*

SLEEP OUT

Be prepared for sleeping in the out-of-doors. Know about proper equipment, shelter, and safety rules.

- Find out about different kinds of sleeping bags. Decide which kind you would buy.
- Find out about different kinds of tents.

- Learn how to pitch a tent and practice doing it.
- Learn knots that are useful for pitching tents, such as the taut line hitch and the bowline (see pages 113–114).
- Read pages 33–50 in *Outdoor Education in Girl Scouting.*
- Learn weather safety rules. Find out about ways to keep your sleeping area and gear as dry as possible.
- Plan an overnight stay in someone's back-yard. Sleep in a sleeping bag.
- Do a night activity that will help you learn about the outdoors. For example:

Practice some astronomy skills. Locate the Big and Little Dippers and the North Star. Or, learn about the sources of the night sounds you hear.

Hang a plain white sheet and shine a light on one side to attract insects.

- Find out about the habits of nocturnal animals (those active at night) in your area.

CAMP OUT

Plan a camping trip. Camping is living in the out-of-doors, not just visiting it.

- Plan menus for well-balanced meals for a two-day camping trip.
- Prepare a checklist of personal items (such as clothing) you would plan to take on an overnight camping trip.
- Earn the Troop Camper badge described in *Girl Scout Badges and Signs*.

Camping Checklist

Use this checklist when preparing for an overnight camping trip. It might help to make up a separate list for things like cooking equipment and sleeping gear. Check off each item as you pack for the trip. (See *Outdoor Education in Girl Scouting* for lists of the types of camping equipment you might need.)

- Adults to help you (be "safety-wise"—have at least one adult for every eight girls)
- Written permission from parent or guardian
- Arrangements for a campsite
- Cooking equipment
- Sleeping gear
- Kaper chart
- First aid kit
- Transportation plans
- Personal items (includes proper clothing and personal hygiene items)
- Schedule of things to do
- Other resources (like money, maps, compass, flashlight, game equipment)

As you explore the out-of-doors, your experience and growing skills will make it possible for you to enjoy more and more opportunities and challenges.

Trips

Going on trips is one of the best parts of being a Junior Girl Scout. You and your Girl Scout friends can take trips for many different reasons—to share good times, to learn about new places and things, to earn badges.

WHERE TO GO

■ ■ ■ ■ ☐ As a Junior Girl Scout, you are old enough to visit many places. For example:

- Biking or hiking trails
- Parks
- Zoos
- Museums
- Your Girl Scout council office
- The town hall or city hall
- A country fair
- Restaurants
- Airports, railroad stations, bus stations
- Libraries
- Synagogues, churches, temples
- Historic places
- Sports centers or arenas (to play or watch—tennis, bowling, softball, etc.)
- Wildlife refuges
- Ice skating rinks
- Farms
- Street fairs or block parties
- Theaters (to see movies, puppet shows, plays)
- A circus

Before you go on any trip, make plans so that everything will go smoothly. At a planning meeting you could talk about:

- Where you will go, and what you will do once you arrive.
- How much it will cost. Will there be admission fees?
- How you will travel. Can you go by one kind of transportation and return by another? How much will it cost?
- What to bring along. Will you travel in uniform? Will you take bag lunches or eat in a restaurant?
- When to take the trip. How long will the trip take? What time must you leave? What time will you return home? How much time do you need for visiting and exploring? Do you need to make reservations or get permission to visit the place?
- What to do in case of rain or other bad weather. Will bad weather change your plans? Should you make another plan just in case?

RESEARCH

■ ■ ☐ Before making a definite decision about where you're going, do some research about some of the possibilities. A trip that sounds rather dull at first may turn out to be exciting when you find out more about it.

Once a decision has been made, find out as much as you can about the place you plan to visit. That information can help you a great deal in your planning. Write or telephone ahead to the place, or write to the Chamber of Commerce of the town or city where you'll be going. The Chamber of Commerce may send you maps or tourist brochures. Most states have their own travel bureaus and will send you a great deal of information about the state. Someone at your local library can help you find the addresses of travel bureaus.

Budgeting

◼ Figure out how much the trip will cost. Make a chart that lists everything you'll have to pay for and how much each thing will cost. Include meals, transportation, equipment and materials, and admission fees. It is a good idea to add some extra money to your final figure just in case your budget estimates were too low.

Permission and Supervision

Before going on a trip, you'll need to get written permission from your parent or guardian. You will also need to have enough adults with you. A Girl Scout book called *Safety-Wise* contains all the safety recommendations that you and your leader will need to know. Work with your leader on planning a safe trip. Your leader will make sure there are permission slips from everyone and a suitable number of adults to come on the trip.

BE A SMART PACKER

◼ Figure out ahead of time what clothing you will need to bring. Pack clothes that will be appropriate for the activities you expect to be doing. It is a good idea to sew name labels in your clothes so they don't get mixed up with other people's clothes. Clothes can be rolled or folded carefully to fit into a suitcase, sleeping bag, or knapsack. Socks and underwear can be stuffed into shoes. Shoes can be placed in paper or plastic bags and then placed in a travel bag.

Put your toothbrush, toothpaste, hairbrush or comb, soap, and other toiletries together in a separate pouch or bag.

Bring along a pillowcase or plastic bag for laundry, in order to keep your dirty clothes separated from your clean ones.

TRAVEL SKILLS

A traveler needs many skills. These include knowing safety procedures (see pages 93–106 in the "Day by Day—Skills for Living" chapter), being able to read certain signs and symbols, knowing how to use maps, and knowing some travel games to help pass the time.

Travel Signs and Symbols

◼◼◻ As you travel, you will see many signs and symbols. Try to learn the meanings of as many as you can. After looking at the signs and symbols on page 159, see if you can decode the story that follows.

Sample Story to Be Decoded

A group of Junior Girl Scouts decided to go camping at a national park. One of the girls had to use a wheelchair because she was unable to walk, so the group wanted to make sure the park had facilities for the ♿ _____. They used the ☎ _____ to call the national park ❓ _____ office to find out about the park's camping facilities.

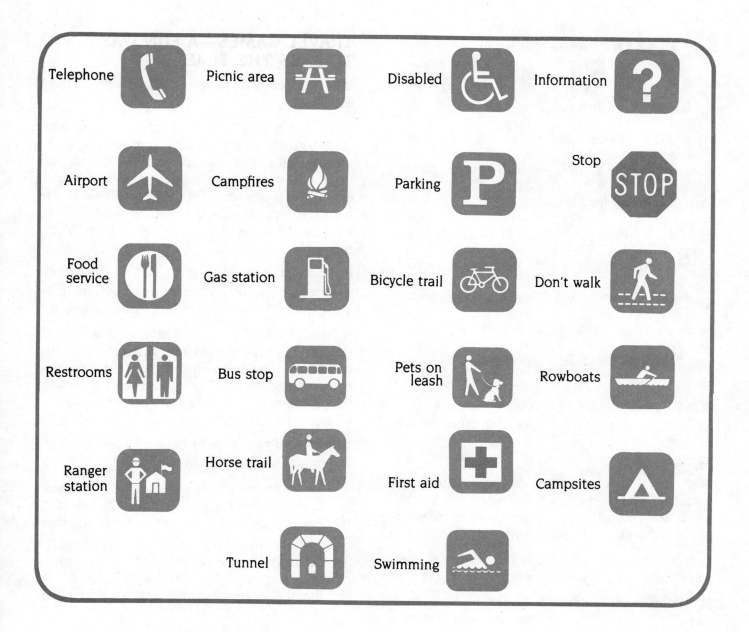

Telephone · Picnic area · Disabled · Information

Airport · Campfires · Parking · Stop

Food service · Gas station · Bicycle trail · Don't walk

Restrooms · Bus stop · Pets on leash · Rowboats

Ranger station · Horse trail · First aid · Campsites

Tunnel · Swimming

The person in the [?] office told them all about the park. It had facilities for the [disabled] with the right kind of [restrooms] and walkways through the woods that could be used by people in wheelchairs.

The park had [campsites], places for [campfires], [picnic area], [swimming], and lots of trails—even a [bicycle trail]. The park sounded perfect for the group.

The girls spent a month planning for the trip—making all their arrangements for meals and equipment, and deciding what things to do when they got there. They made sure to pack two [first aid] to take with them.

On the morning of their departure, they left at 8:00 A.M. Their leader took half of the girls in her car, and the co-leader took the other half in her van. As they were leaving their town, they passed the ✈ and a 🚌, where a lot of people were waiting to get on the bus. There was a 🛑, and the traffic light was flashing 🚶. The girls were glad to be going camping and to have a change from town living for a while.

After traveling for an hour, they went through a 🚇 and saw a sign indicating that they had reached the national park. Everyone was happy to finally be there. The leader and co-leader drove to the 🅿 and parked the car and van.

■■□ Find out about other travel symbols. Have fun making up your own stories for other people to figure out.

Maps

■■ Learn how to use a map. Get a map of the place that you plan to visit and figure out exactly which way you will travel to get there. Remember to bring the map with you on your trip.

Sometimes, if you're on a long trip, it's fun to play some map games. Here are a few:

■ **Animals and colors** Look at a map and find as many places as you can that have colors or animal names in them (such as Yellowstone National Park or Buffalo).

■ **Last letter first** You need at least two people for this game. One person finds a name of a place on a map and says it out loud (for example, "Dallas"). The next person has to find a place on the map that begins with the last letter of the other person's place (for example, "San Francisco"; it begins with "s," the last letter of "Dallas"). Take turns until you've run out of names.

TRAVEL GAMES—A FUN WAY TO PASS THE TIME

■■□ To make your trip more fun, try some of these activities.

TRIP SCRAPBOOK LOG Collect items for a scrapbook log of your trip. Tickets, souvenirs, and pictures can all go in the scrapbook. While on the trip, make notes about the highlights of your experiences. When you return home, you will be able to put together a scrapbook to look at whenever you want to remember the fun things you did on the trip.

COUNTING CARS Pick out a type of car (station wagon, pick-up truck, limousine, etc.). As you travel along, find as many cars of this type as you can.

NUMBERS Find two of something. Look for anything that is in pairs (two birds flying together, two people standing on a corner together, two hourses or cows standing together). Try the same game with threes, fours, or fives. The higher the number, the greater the challenge!

TRIP LAP DESK Make a desk that you can write and draw on while traveling.

1. Find a box that is big enough to fit on your lap. It should be at least 10 inches (25 cm) high, 10 inches (25 cm) wide, and 15 inches (38 cm) long.

2. Carefully cut the flaps off the top. Save the flaps. Cut a half-circle out of one of the sides where your legs can fit through. You should be able to pull the desk over your lap.

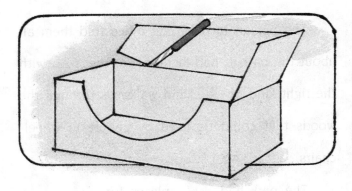

3. Glue the flaps around the solid bottom of the box, which will be the desktop, so that the flaps stick up about a half-inch (1.5 cm) above the box.

This will make a ridge so that pens and pencils won't roll off.

4. Decorate the box. It's now ready to use on your next trip!

MORE TRAVEL TIPS AND A REMINDER LIST

1. If you have a ticket for your trip that needs to be confirmed, call the ticket office ahead of time to confirm your seat and the time of departure.

2. Pack lightly. Take only things that you can carry easily and that you're almost sure to need. Choose clothes that you can wash and wear without ironing.

3. Be prepared for the weather. Make sure your clothes will be suitable for the type of weather where you're going.

4. Make sure you have enough money for your trip.

5. Allow plenty of time to get to your transportation so that you have time to take care of your luggage, find departure gates, go to the bathroom, etc.

6. Wear comfortable shoes.

7. If you suffer from motion sickness, it's better to ride in a seat next to a window. Looking out the window can help keep you from getting sick.

8. Use seat belts.

9. Eat balanced meals when you travel. Too much junk food or snacks can affect your digestive system and spoil your fun on the trip.

10. Do your part to make the trip go smoothly by being a helpful traveler. Be patient with others. Play with travelers who are bored or cranky. Help keep the vehicle in which you are traveling clean and neat.

11. Write thank-you notes to the people who have helped you with your trip.

CHAPTER 10

Bridging to Cadette Girl Scouting

Moving from one Girl Scout age level to another is called bridging. You will bridge from Junior to Cadette Girl Scouting at the end of your last year as a Junior Girl Scout. If you have already bridged from one Girl Scout age level to another, you know the basics of bridging.

Helping Brownie Girl Scouts Bridge to Junior Girl Scouting

During all the time you are a Junior Girl Scout, you will be able to help Brownie Girl Scouts with their

bridging. One way of doing this is to work to earn the Junior Aide patch (see page 201 in *Girl Scout Badges and Signs*). Some other ways are:

- Wear your Junior Girl Scout uniform to a Brownie Girl Scout meeting and tell the girls about the Junior Girl Scout patches, badges, and pins.
- Become a pen pal to a Brownie Girl Scout and keep her up-to-date about what you are doing in Girl Scouting.
- Go on a trip with Brownie Girl Scouts.
- Help at Brownie Girl Scout meetings.
- Help Brownie Girl Scouts plan their bridging ceremony.

Becoming a Cadette Girl Scout

You've had a lot of fun and learned a great deal as a Junior Girl Scout. When you become a Cadette Girl Scout, opportunities for new achievements, relationships, and adventures await you! You will have more freedom and responsibility as you create goals and plans to guide your activities. You will discover more about yourself, further build your skills for independent living, go to new places, and meet many interesting people.

To help you in becoming a Cadette Girl Scout, you might take part in bridging activities during your last year as a Junior Girl Scout. By doing at least one activity from each of the eight bridging steps described in this chapter, you can earn the Bridge to Cadette Girl Scouts patch. (See page 170.) You might also do other activities that you think of yourself for each bridging step.

BRIDGING STEP 1: FIND OUT ABOUT CADETTE GIRL SCOUTING

- Look through the resources for Cadette Girl Scouts—the *Cadette and Senior Girl Scout Handbook, Cadette and Senior Girl Scout Interest Projects*, and *From Dreams to Reality: Career Cards*.
- Fill in the "Now I Am" chart on page 21 in the *Cadette and Senior Girl Scout Handbook*.
- Find out about the Girl Scout Silver Award.
- Find out about the uniforms and recognitions for Cadette Girl Scouts.
- Look at *Wider Ops: Girl Scout Wider Opportunities* to find out about opportunities that Cadette Girl Scouts might be qualified for.
- Talk with a Cadette or Senior Girl Scout who has been on a wider opportunity.
- Find out about the Reader's Digest Foundation Grants for community service.
- Invite a girl who is a Cadette to tell you about Cadette Girl Scouting.
- Find a Cadette or Senior Girl Scout who can help you with bridging activities.

———————————————————

———————————————————

———————————————————

———————————————————

What I learned: ———————————————

———————————————————

———————————————————

———————————————————

Date completed: ————————————

BRIDGING STEP 2: DO A CADETTE GIRL SCOUT ACTIVITY

- Do an activity from the *Cadette and Senior Girl Scout Handbook*.
- Do an activity from *Cadette and Senior Girl Scout Interest Projects*.
- Do a career exploration activity found in Chapter 6 of the *Cadette and Senior Girl Scout Handbook*.

What I did: _____

_____

_____

_____

Date completed: _____

BRIDGING STEP 3: DO SOMETHING WITH A CADETTE GIRL SCOUT

- Be an international pen pal to a girl who is between twelve and fourteen years old.
- Go on a field trip.
- Learn how to use an outdoor stove.
- Do a service project.
- Do an art or science project.
- Plan a menu for an outdoor camping trip.
- Do a flag ceremony.
- Work with a Leader-in-Training to plan an activity that will be done with Daisy Girl Scouts.

Name(s) of the Cadette Girl Scout(s) I worked with:

_____

_____

_____

_____

What we did together: _____

_____

_____

_____

_____

Date completed: _____

BRIDGING STEP 4: SHARE WHAT YOU LEARN ABOUT CADETTE GIRL SCOUTING WITH JUNIOR, BROWNIE, OR DAISY GIRL SCOUTS

- Teach them something you learned about Cadette Girl Scouting.
- Tell them about a field trip or service project that you did with a Cadette Girl Scout.
- Tell them about a wider opportunity that a Cadette Girl Scout went on.
- Show them pictures of the Cadette Girl Scout uniform and tell them about the recognitions that Cadette Girl Scouts can earn.

Names of the girls I shared information with: ____

_____

_____

_____

What I did: _____

_____

_____

_____

Date completed: _____

BRIDGING STEP 5: DO CADETTE GIRL SCOUT RECOGNITION ACTIVITIES

- Earn a Dabbler interest project patch for one of the worlds of interest, as described in *Cadette and Senior Girl Scout Interest Projects*.
- Earn an interest project patch by doing one of the following projects from *Cadette and Senior Girl Scout Interest Projects*

  Child Care
  Sports
  Invitation to the Dance
  Hi-Tech Communication
  Eco-Action
- Do an interest project activity from each world of interest in *Cadette and Senior Girl Scout Interest Projects*.
- Do three activities in Chapter 6 of the *Cadette and Senior Girl Scout Handbook*.

What I did: _____

_____

_____

_____

Date completed: _____

BRIDGING STEP 6: TAKE ON A LEADERSHIP ROLE

- Teach safety rules to younger children.
- Teach others to make something.
- Do activity #1 in the Leadership interest project in *Cadette and Senior Girl Scout Interest Projects*.
- Help recruit Girl Scout members for your Girl Scout council.
- Earn the Junior Aide patch (see *Girl Scout Badges and Signs*).
- Assist the leader of a group of younger Girl Scouts.

What I did: _____

_____

_____

_____

_____

Date completed: _____

BRIDGING STEP 7: HELP PLAN YOUR BRIDGING CEREMONY

- Learn how to do an opening or closing for your ceremony that is different from any opening or closing you have done before.
- Do a Girl Scouts' Own ceremony.
- Write a special poem about Junior or Cadette Girl Scouting.
- Compose a song for your ceremony.
- Design and make special invitations for your bridging ceremony.
- Make decorations to be used at your bridging ceremony.

What I did: _____

_____

_____

_____

Date completed: _____

What our bridging ceremony was like (when it was, who was invited, and what happened): _____

_____

_____

_____

_____

Date completed: _____

BRIDGING STEP 8: PLAN AND DO A SUMMER GIRL SCOUT ACTIVITY

(You may be able to get your Bridge to Cadette Girl Scouts patch before the summer. But, be sure to do this step over the summer.)

- Go to a Girl Scout camp.
- Do a summer service project.
- Plan an all-day outing with some other Girl Scouts.
- Plan and hold an outdoor slumber party.
- Plan and have a campfire.

What I (we) did: _____

_____

_____

_____

Date completed: _____

Bridge to Cadette Girl Scouts Patch

The activities for this patch will help you to find out about some of the fun and adventures that await you when you become a Cadette Girl Scout. You must complete at least one activity in each of the eight steps described in this chapter. Keep track of what you do by filling in the record of your bridging activities in the blank spaces on pages 164–170.

Keeping Track of Your Junior Girl Scout Friends

Some of your friends may be going with you into Cadette Girl Scouting; others may be continuing in Junior Girl Scouting. Use the space below to collect these girls' autographs, notes, or poems—or whatever else they may want to write. You'll enjoy looking back at this page when you're a Cadette Girl Scout.

CHAPTER 11

Junior Girl Scout Recognitions

In choosing Girl Scout program activities, you will naturally pick those topics that sound most interesting to you. If you find, upon exploring a subject further, that it interests you a great deal, you might decide to complete a Junior Girl Scout badge or sign related to the subject.

Junior Girl Scout badges and signs are recognitions that you can earn by developing new skills or learning more about a subject. These recognitions are symbols of your accomplishments. You may wear them on your Junior Girl Scout uniform sash, as a reminder of all that you have done and as a way of letting others know about what subjects you find most interesting.

Junior Girl Scout Badges

There are 88 Girl Scout badges covering many different subjects. Seventy-nine of these badges are described in *Girl Scout Badges and Signs*, and include activities that you can do either alone or with other girls. In this section of the handbook, you will find nine badge topics. Many of the badge activities should be completed with others who are also interested in the topic. Under the name for each badge, you will find directions telling how many activities must be completed to earn the recognition.

LEADERSHIP

Complete four activities.

1. Organize a leadership group in your school or neighborhood. Ask teachers or the school principal to speak with you and your friends about ways your group might help students in the school. Invite an adult to help you plan and carry out some type of program that will involve meeting at least four times.

    Some program ideas are:
    - ☐ a tutoring program
    - ☐ a safety awareness program
    - ☐ an after-school sports program
    - ☐ games for lunch recess period

2. With a group of friends, organize two of these activities. (See pages 67–68 in the "Leadership and Groups" chapter.)
    - ☐ Partner
    - ☐ Weekend Best
    - ☐ Favorites

3. Make a list of the ways you are a leader. Then compare your list with the "Leaders . . ." list on page 67. Decide on some skills or abilities that leaders have and that you would like to develop in yourself. Come up with a plan for becoming a better leader, and then put the plan into action.

4. Become a big sister to a younger girl who doesn't have one. Teach her some games and songs, help her with homework, and help her learn safety and first aid tips.

5. Organize a fan club for your favorite performing artist. Find at least four friends who would like to be part of the club. Read pages 65–68 in the "Leadership and Groups" chapter to learn about ways to help the group work well together.

6. Find out about and become involved in a campaign in your community. For example, the campaign might relate to:
    - ☐ Seat belt laws
    - ☐ A voting drive
    - ☐ Relief aid to other countries
    - ☐ Missing children
    - ☐ Drunk driving laws

7. Plan and carry out a simple service project with others. Read pages 72–73, "Service in Girl Scouting," to help you with your work.

LOOKING YOUR BEST

Complete five activities.

10/9/91 1. Plan and carry out a hairstyle party. Learn how to do at least one hairstyle that is different from your own. Try it on yourself or on a volunteer. Share hair care tips. Find a shampoo and a conditioner that are good for your type of hair. Share information about the proper use of the products.

12/11/91 2. Put on a fashion show with a theme. Some themes you might consider are outdoor fashion, fashion through history, future fashion, hot weather wear.

12/11/91 3. Help a group of younger girls learn about personal care. Include subjects like caring for clothing and selecting outfits to wear, as well as personal hygiene.

10/9/91 4. Find out about careers in industries related to fashion and appearance. Interview people who work as department store buyers, fashion consultants, fashion designers, hair stylists, or cosmetologists.

   OR Collect newspaper or magazine stories about people who work in this field.

5. Make an article of clothing for yourself, or for someone else. It can be hand- or machine-sewn, knitted, crocheted, or even macraméd.

6. Learn the basic embroidery stitches described on pages 140–141 in the "Creative Explorations" chapter. Then, together with some friends, use the stitches to do a group project. You could make something for a special person or group. For example, you might embroider a "Quiet, Please" sign for the local library, or a wall hanging with the Girl Scout Promise for your troop meeting place.

10/14/91 7. Make an accessory that matches your favorite outfit or that you can give to someone else as a gift. It might be a necklace, hairpins or barrettes, or a bracelet.

8. Plan a group health feast. Have each person prepare one type of healthy food to bring to the feast to share. Then, enjoy! See the section on nutrition on pages 91–93 to help you with your planning.

COMMUNICATION

Complete six activities.

1. Create a new language that you can use to communicate with someone else. You could use numbers, symbols, designs, or pictures to stand for letters or words. Teach your new language to others.

2. Learn how to say things in other languages. Try to talk with someone who knows a different language. Have the person help you pronounce words correctly.

3. Study the sign language alphabet. Learn to sign your name and say "Hello," "I am a Girl Scout," "Thank you," "Have a nice day," and "Good-bye." See page 76 for information.

4. Carry out a body language study. Make a list of different movements, postures, and expressions you have seen. For example, think about the positions people sit in, the gestures they make, the expressions on their faces. Next to each movement, posture, or expression, write the message it may send to others. For example, someone who puts one hand up to her forehead may be sending the message "I am thinking hard."

OR Play a game of charades, using only body language to convey a message.

5. Start a newsletter or short magazine. Include pictures, drawings, and cartoons along with the written items. To help you think of ways to arrange your information, look at magazines and newspapers. "Publish" your newsletter at least four times.

6. Find out about how advertisements are used to sell a product. Look at two or more different types of advertisements—on television, on the radio, in a magazine, or in a newspaper. What are the advertised products supposed to do? What messages are communicated by the slogans, skits, music, and people in the advertisements? See the consumer section in the "Day by Day—Skills for Living" chapter (page 109) for some information.

OR Study the packaging of products. Look at several packages and think about the colors, sizes, shapes, and designs that were used. Do certain colors tend to be used for certain types of products? What do you think packaging has to do with selling products? Does packaging affect the success of a product? Share your findings with others.

7. With two or more friends, make up a short story that will have sound effects when it is read. Use a tape recorder to record the story and the sounds. For example, if a line in the story says that "someone knocked at the door," record a knocking sound as part of the story. Play the recording for others.

8. Lay an outdoor trail for others to follow. Read pages 116–118, on trail markers and mapping directions, to help you.

9. Make and carry out a "peer pact." See page 50 in the "Relationships" chapter.

HELPING IN YOUR COMMUNITY 10/92

Complete four activities.

✓ 1. Work with others to help organize an animal safety program in your community. Find out about what procedures your local animal shelter has established for finding and caring for abandoned dogs and cats. Also, find out how people can register their pets and about the vaccinations that animals need. Make posters, signs, and handouts to share this information with people in your community.

✓ 2. Run a clean-up-your-community campaign. Pick an area that has a litter problem and organize a group to clean it up. Post a sign that says "Another Good Job Completed by Girl Scouts."

✓ 3. Make tape recordings of children's stories for blind children or for children too young to read. Select stories that you like and practice reading them out loud. Donate the tapes to a library, school, or other community organization.

OR Organize a story hour at the local library.

4. Form a homework help group. Each person in the group can donate time each week, for a period of at least one month, to help another student with schoolwork.

✓ 5. Plan and carry out a project, such as a clothing collection drive, to help those in need. Donate the items to an organization in your community. *Bike-a-thon*

6. Find out ways you can work with others to help senior citizens in your community. Help for at least one week.

7. Plan a personal safety workshop. Read "Safety Do's and Don'ts" on pages 93–98. Make posters and give skits that show others how to stay safe.

HEALTHY LIVING

Complete six activities.

1. Do three of the "Knowing People Better" activities listed on page 46.

2. Do two of the food tests described on pages 92–93 in the "Day by Day—Skills for Living" chapter.

3. Prepare a first aid kit for your home or Girl Scout meeting place. Include a list of emergency phone numbers. Read pages 98–104 in the "Day by Day"—Skills for Living" chapter.

4. With the help of a trained adult, organize an exercise class for other girls your age. Demonstrate and teach activities that can be used to warm up, work out, and cool down. See pages 38–41 in the "Who Am I?" chapter for some ideas.

5. Find out about the effects of smoking, drugs, and alcohol. Use this information to make booklets that will help others learn.

6. Plants can help to make a healthy environment. With a group, build a large terrarium. For at least one month, keep a record of how the plants grow. If possible, compare these plants with plants that have not been kept in the terrarium. In making your comparison, consider appearance, size, and amount of growth over the one-month period.

7. Take the Values Quiz on pages 25–26. Ask three other people to take the quiz as well. Explain the results to them.

8. Read "Group Sports" and "Team Sports" on pages 135–137. Complete the activities for at least two different sports.

TECHNOLOGY

Complete five activities.

1. Play the technology game "I Can Live Without It" (see page 150).

2. Learn about one product or invention that has improved the way things are done in the home or on the farm. Find out what was used in its place 10, 40, and 80 years ago. Write a story (or use pictures) to show how the product has changed.

3. Find out some ways in which technology has affected the medical services in your community. Invite someone in the medical field to talk to your group about new types of technology.

OR Make a display picture of a person that shows which body parts can sometimes be replaced with machines or artificial parts. Explain to others how the machines or artificial parts work.

4. Find out what steps would be necessary in order to have a career as an astronaut.

5. Build something by using at least three different tools. See pages 109–111 in the "Day by Day—Skills for Living" chapter for information.

6. Complete the "Think Like a Computer" activity on page 150. Share your chart with others.

7. Trace the source of the water that you use in your home—from the kitchen faucet back to where the water was originally found in nature. Find out the location of the reservoir in your community, how water gets into the reservoir, and how it is purified.

YOUR OUTDOOR SURROUNDINGS

Complete six activities.

1. Make a work of art using natural objects that you have found. Be sure not to disturb living creatures or plants.

2. Visit a playground or park and watch children at play. Take notes about any activities they are doing that are unsafe. Use your notes to make a list of safety do's and don'ts for Brownie and Daisy Girl Scouts. Organize a Safe Fun day that includes teaching outdoor games to younger girls.

3. Find out about the habits of an insect by keeping and observing it for two weeks. Build a home that is something like its natural home and provide it with food. Write about the things you observe. After you finish your observations, return the insect to its natural surroundings.

OR Find out what types of food ants like to eat. Pick a site where you have seen ants and locate an anthill for your study. Bring along small scraps of different types of food. Arrange the food in a circle around the anthill, making sure that the items are all the same distance from each other and are all about 12 inches (30 cm.) from the anthill. Sit quietly and watch. Make a record of the things you observe. For example, note down which foods the ants find first, which ones they eat first, whether the ants eat the foods there or carry them home.

4. Plan and carry out a theme hike for three people or more. Try to have the hike last a full morning or afternoon. See pages 111–114 in the "Day by Day—Skills for Living" chapter and pages 153–154 in the "Creative Explorations" chapter for information and ideas.

5. Learn how to use a compass. Read "Finding Directions with a Compass" on page 117 to help you. You can make your own compass if you want. See pages 150–152 for directions.

6. Work with at least one other person to make miniature landfills for garbage. Each person makes her own landfill. Use a clear plastic glass or container. Put soil in the container. Bury small pieces of garbage under the soil. Use a variety of items like pieces of food, plastic, cardboard, and aluminum foil. Make sure you can see the garbage pressed up against the sides of the container. Store the container outdoors where it can be exposed to the weather. Keep a record of the changes that take place in the garbage and the soil. After three weeks, compare your findings with the findings of others. Observe and compare again after three more weeks.

7. Learn to tie three of the knots described on pages 113–114 in the "Day by Day—Skills for Living" chapter.

8. Interview three people who work at different jobs in the out-of-doors. Find out the main things they do and what they like and dislike about their jobs. If possible, visit the places where they work.

WIDER OPPORTUNITIES
Complete five activities.

1. Invite a Cadette or Senior Girl Scout to talk to you and your friends about a wider opportunity she has been on.

   OR Invite someone from your council to talk to your group about wider opportunities. Find out which events and workshops you can attend as a Junior Girl Scout.

2. Plan a budget and packing list for a one-week trip to a place you would like to visit. The budget should include the costs for transportation, meals, admission fees, souvenirs, and anything else you are likely to buy. The packing list should include clothing appropriate for the climate and suited for the activities you have planned. Share your budget and packing list with others.

3. Make a brochure of special places to visit in your area. Visit three or more different tourist attractions and historical sites with your friends. Take notes and pictures at each location to share with others.

4. Learn about wider opportunities now being offered by councils. Ask your Girl Scout leader to bring her copy of *Wider Ops: Girl Scout Wider Opportunities* to a troop meeting. Look through it and decide on three wider opportunities you would like to participate in. Make a list of the requirements, cost, location, and any special equipment you would need.

   OR Design a make-believe wider opportunity. Describe where it would take place, how long it would last, what activities would be done, the number of participants, and special requirements and equipment.

5. Organize a travel conference. Each girl picks a country she would like to visit and finds out as much as she can by using resources such as books, magazines, television documentaries, travel agents, people who are from the country, and people who have traveled to the country. Share this information at the travel conference.

6. Design a wider opportunity for a group of younger Girl Scouts. Working with other Junior Girl Scouts and Girl Scout leaders, find out what wider opportunities younger girls would like and would be able to do. Then plan, research, and carry out an appropriate wider opportunity for a sister Daisy or Brownie Girl Scout troop. Make sure you involve the Girl Scout leaders in the activity and that you have all the permissions that you need.

7. Find out what information is recorded in a passport. Make your own make-believe passport.

CAREERS

Complete five activities.

1. With a group, make career and interest/talent cards. See page 125 in the "Hopes and Dreams" chapter.

2. Find out about at least five jobs that you can get without going to college. What type of training, clothes, tools, and equipment are used for each job? Talk to women who have these jobs. What do they do on a typical day? What skills do they have? What do they like and dislike about their work?

OR Find out about at least five jobs that require a college education or advanced training. Complete the activity as described above.

3. Make a collage using pictures of workers. Select a variety of occupations. Try to include pictures of people at work who are wearing uniforms or using their on-the-job equipment. See page 10 in *Careers to Explore for Brownie and Junior Girl Scouts.*

4. Plan a Career Discovery evening or afternoon. Invite guest speakers or show films.

5. Make a family career tree. See pages 126–127 in the "Hopes and Dreams" chapter.

6. Collect newspaper or magazine stories that tell about women athletes or politicians in your community, in other cities or states, or in different countries.

7. Organize a trip to a workplace. Talk to the workers and find out about their tasks and their responsibilities.

Junior Girl Scout Signs

You can earn four signs as a Junior Girl Scout: the Sign of the Rainbow, the Sign of the Sun, the Sign of the Satellite, and the Sign of the World. The activities required for each of these signs will help you to learn more about yourself and your community. The requirements include doing badge activities and a service project. **A badge or badge activity can only be used once in completing any of the signs.** Note that it may take several months to earn each sign.

The Signs of the Rainbow, the Sun, and the Satellite are described in *Girl Scout Badges and Signs*. The Sign of the World is described below.

SIGN OF THE WORLD

Millions of people live on this earth—and everyone can contribute, in some way, toward making our world a better place. By completing the activities required for this sign, you can do something to improve your world. You can also get to know yourself better, increase your understanding of your own values, and gain experience in working with others.

I. Complete two badges in the badge section of this handbook (pages 172–183) and one badge from the World of People in *Girl Scout Badges and Signs*.

I earned these badges: _____

_____

II. Complete five activities in the "Relationships" chapter of this handbook.

Here is what I did: _____

_____

_____

_____

III. Complete four activities in the "People" chapter of this handbook.

I did these four activities: _____

_____

IV. Read pages 25–28 in the "Who Am I?" chapter in this handbook. Then do the values activities in that section.

Here are some things that I learned by reading:

_____

_____

_____

_____

Here are some things that I found out about myself by completing the values activities: _____

_____

_____

_____

V. Plan your own service project and carry it out.

Here is what I did: _____

_____

_____

_____

_____

My signature   Date Sign of the World completed

_____

Signature of an adult who reviewed what I did.

Index

Accidents, 99–102
Adults, 52
Aerobic dance, 39–40
Alcohol, 88
American flag, handling of, 15–17
American Indian (Native American), 75
American Indian Corn Pudding, 81
Arts:
    literary, 142–143
    performing, 143–144
    visual, 138–142

Baden-Powell, Sir Robert, 18
Badge activities, 172–183
Basketball, 136–137
Big Dipper, 117
Bites, animal, 99
Bleeding, 99
Blisters, 99
Braille, 82
Brainstorming (in troop planning), 70
Bridge to Cadette Girl Scouts patch, 13
Bridging ceremony, 14
    Junior Girl Scout to Cadette, 164–170
Brownie Girl Scout, 11
    bridging to Junior Girl Scout, 163
    participation and bridging patches, 13
    Try-Its, 13
    wings, 13
Buddy Burner, 155
Budgeting, 107–108
    on trips, 158
Bumps and bruises, 99
Burns, 100

Cadette and Senior Girl Scout Handbook (book), 164, 165, 167
Cadette and Senior Girl Scout Interest Projects (book), 164, 165, 167, 168
Cadette Girl Scout, 11
Camp of Tomorrow, 8
Camp Out, 157
Canciones de Nuestra Cabaña (Songs of Our Cabaña) (book), 144
Candlelight ceremony, 14
Careers:
    badge activities for, 183
    choosing, 125–127
    and hobbies, 31, 126
Careers to Explore for Brownie and Junior Girl Scouts (book), 183
Catch board (tool project), 111
Ceremonies, Girl Scout, 14–17
Chanoyu (tea ceremony), 79
Chinese New Year, 77
Chinese Velvet Corn Soup, 81

Choking, 100
Cigarettes, 88
Clothing, 88–91
Color pictures, creating, 138
Colors, 149
Communication, badge activities, 175–176
Community, badge activities in, 177
Compass:
    badge activities with, 180
    construction of, 150–151
    use of, 117
Computers, 153
Consumer awareness activities, 109, 175
Cookie sale, 72
Cook Out, 154–156
Cooking, international, 81–82
Copper cleaner, making, 152
Cool-down exercises, 40–41, 132
Council strip, 13
Councils, Girl Scout, 5–6
Court of Awards, 14
Court of Honor, 69, 70

Daisy Girl Scout, 11
Dance, 144
    aerobic, 39
Daydreaming, 121–122
Decision chart, 57–58
Decision-making, seven steps, 59–61
Decoupage, 142
Diet, balanced, 92
Directions, by star-gazing, 116–117
Disabled, 82–84
Discussing and disagreeing, 45
Double Dutch (jump rope), 135–136
Dream Box, 70
Dreidel (toy), 78
Drugs, 88

Edith Macy Conference Center, 8
Elderly, 82
Embroidery, 140–141, 174
Emergencies, 99–104
Emergency phone numbers, 103
Endurance, 37–38
Executive Board system (troop government), 70
Exercises, 37–41
    cool-down, 40–41
    for endurance, flexibility, and strength, 37
    warm-up, 38–39
    work-out, 39–40
Explore Out, 153–154
Eye injuries, 100

Fainting, 101
Family, 46–47
    career tree of, 126–127
Feelings, 31–33
    within family, 47
Festivals, multicultural, 78–80
Fire safety, 104–106
First aid, 98–102, 178
Fitness, physical, 36–41
Flag ceremony, 14–17
Flexibility, physical, 36–37
Fly-Up Ceremony, 14
Folk music and dance, 144
Food:
    groups, four basic, 91–92
    tests for nutrients in, 92–93
Founder's Day, 20
Fractures, sprains, and broken bones, 101
Friends, 50–52
Friendship circle, 9–10
Friendship squeeze, 3
Frisbee, 134
From Dreams to Reality: Career Cards (book), 164
Frostbite, 101

Games, for groups, 67–68
Girl Scout:
    ceremonies, 14–17
    handshake, 9
    insignia and recognitions, 1, 12–13
    Law, 2–4, 15
    leaders, 5–6
    motto, 10
    pin, 13
    Promise, 2, 15
    service projects, 2, 10, 72–73, 173
    sign, 9
    slogan, 10
    special days, 20
    strip, 13
    traditions, 9–10
    troops, 5–6, 11
    uniform, 12
Girl Scout Badges and Signs (book), 2, 12, 132, 163, 165, 172, 184
Girl Scout People Pyramid, 4–7
Girl Scout Pocket Songbook (book), 144
Girl Scout Silver Award, 164
Girl Scout Week, 19
Girl Scouting, worldwide:
    birthday of, 20
    interesting facts about, 19
    world centers, 8

Girl Scouts of the U.S.A., 5–7
  age levels, 11–12
  badges, 13
  bridging, 12
  cookie sale, 72
  councils, 5–6
  national centers, 7–8
Girl Scouts' Own, 14, 168
Goal planning, 123–124
Groups, 53–54
  changes in, 67
  games for, 67–68
Gymnastics, 134–135

Haiku poetry, 79
Hair care, 86–87
Hannukah, 77–78
Healthy living, badge activities in, 178
Hobbies, 30–31
  and careers, 31, 126
Home decorating, 129–132
Human body, understanding of, 33–41
Hungarian Korozot Dip, 81–82
Hygiene, personal, 86–87, 174
Hyperthermia (too much body heat), 101
Hypothermia (too little body heat), 101

Image book (scrapbook), 23
India, mosaics of, 80
Individual Sports Word Find, 133
Insect bites, stings, 101
Insignia and recognitions, 1, 12–13
Investiture ceremony, 14

Jacknife, 114–115
Juggling, 136
Juliette Gordon Low Federal Complex, 19
Juliette Gordon Low Girl Scout National Center, 7–8
Juliette Low World Friendship Fund, 19
Junior Aide patch, 13
Junior Girl Scout, 1–2, 11
  badges, 172–185
  bridging to Cadette Girl Scouts, 164–170
Junior Girl Scout signs, 13, 184–185
Junior Girl Scout Handbook, 1–2

Kaper chart, 3, 72
Knots, 113–114, 181
Kwanza (holiday festival), 77

Languages, foreign, 76
Leaders, Girl Scout, 5–6
Leadership, 66–67, 173
  and troop government, 69–70
Literary arts, 142–143
Look Out, 153
Lou Henry Hoover memorials, 154
Low, Juliette Gordon ("Daisy"), 17–19

Macramé, 130–131
Map-making, 117–118
Maps, reading, 160
Math, 144–153
Meet Out, 153
Membership star and disc, 13
Menstruation, 36
Mini-World Conference, 82
Money management, 106–109
Mosaic, 80
Move Out, 153
Mural painting, 138
Music, 144

Nigeria, tie-dye of, 79
North Star (Polaris), 117
Nosebleed, 101
Nutrition, 91–93, 174

Olave House, 8
Optical illusions, 148, 149
Our Cabaña, 8
Our Chalet, 8
Outdoor:
  activities, 30
  adventures, 111–118
  badge activities in, 180–181
  explorations, 153–157
  skills, 113–118
Outdoor Education in Girl Scouting (book), 118, 156, 157

Painting, mural, 138
Paper-mache, 139
Paper-making, 142
Patrol leader cord, 69–70
Patrol systems (troop government), 69–70
Pen pals, 52
  international, 82
"Peer pact," 50
Peers and peer pressure, 47–50
Performing arts, 143–144
Phone numbers, emergency, 103

Photography, 139–140
Physical fitness, 36–41
Planning, four steps in, 70–72
Plants, 129–139
Plays, 143–144
Pledge of Allegiance, 15
Poisoning, 102
Printmaking, 138–139
Puberty, 35–36
Pulse rate, measuring, 35
Puzzles, 147–149

Quiet sign, 9
Quilting, 80

Recipes, international, 81–82
Recognitions, 1, 12–13
Rededication ceremony, 14
Riddles, 147, 148
Role models, 126
Role-playing, 45

Safety, 93–98
  do's and don't's, 93–97
  outdoors, 112
  with fire, 104–106
  with tools, 110
"Safety sense," 93
Safety-Wise (book), 158
Sangam, 8
School, 124–125
Science, 144–153
Self-esteem (the one and only me), 22–23
Senior Girl Scout, 11
Service projects, 2, 10, 72–73, 173
Sewing, 89–91
  kit, 89
Sharing and listening, 45
Shock, 102
Sign language, 76, 175
Sign of the World, 184–185
Sign of the Rainbow, 184
Sign of the Satellite, 184
Sign of the Sun, 184
Sing Together (book), 144
Skin care, 87–88
Sleep Out, 156
Splinter, 102
Sports, 132–137
  as hobby, 30
  group, 135–136
  individual, 133–134
  team, 136–137

Sports equipment, 137
Strength, physical, 37
Sunburn, 102
Suzy Safety, 20

Talents, 29–30
Technology, 150–153
  badge activities in, 179
Teeth care, 87
Thermos bottle, making, 152–153
Thinking Day, 19, 20
Three Kings Day, 77
Tie-dye, 79
Time, and making decisions, 63
Tools, 109–111
Town meeting system (troop
    government), 70
Tracy's Column, 32–33
Traditions:
  family, 76
  Girl Scout, 9–10
Trail markers, 116, 176

Travel:
  games, 160–161
  packing for, 158
  research about, 157–158
  signs and symbols, 158–160, 175
  skills, 158–160, 161
Trefoil pin, 12
"Trekkers," 7
Trips, 157–161
  to workplaces, 126
Troop, 5–6
  dues, 72, 108–109
  government, 11, 69–70
  number and crest, 13
  planning activities (four steps),
    70–72

"Umoja" (holiday value), 77
Uniform, Girl Scout, 12
United States:
  folk arts in, 80
  heritage of, 75–76

Vagabond Stove, 154
Values, 25–28, 178
Values quiz, 25–26
Visual arts, 138–142

Warm-up exercises, 38–39, 132
Weather, and safety, 96
Wider opportunities, badge activities
    in, 182
Wider Ops: Girl Scout Wider Opportunities
    (book), 7, 164, 182
Work-out (exercise), 39–40
World Association of Girl Guides and
    Girl Scouts (WAGGGS), 6–7
World Association pin, 12, 13
World of People, 20
World of the Arts, 20
World of the Out-of-Doors, 20
World of Today and Tomorrow, 20
World of Well-Being, 20
Worlds of Interest, 20

Yoga, 40–41

GREYSCALE

BIN TRAVELER FORM

Cut By _Dina Lopez_ Qty _36_ Date _09-04_

Scanned By _____ Qty _____ Date _____

Scanned Batch IDs

_____ _____ _____

Notes / Exception

_____

_____

_____

_____

_____